The Magik of
Lucifer

Harnessing Four Powerful Aspects

David Thompson

High Magik Book 12

The Magik of

Lucifer

Harnessing Four Powerful Aspects

David Thompson

High Magik Book 12

Trans Mundane Publishing
Occult Knowledge

ISBN: 9781961765160 Paperback

Dust Cover Image: File ID169761374 | © Creativehearts Dreamstime.com
Inner image Photo 59717607 © Creativehearts | Dreamstime.com

Cover design by David Thompson

A Legal Disclaimer:

By Law, I am obliged to let you know that this is for entertainment purposes only and does not claim to prevent or cure any diseases. The advice in this book should not be construed as financial, medical, or psychological advice. Please seek such advice from a professional.

By purchasing this book, and working the rituals, you understand that results are not guaranteed. In light of this and in the unlikely event that this course does not work for you or, in the very unlikely event, this book causes physical harm to you or a loved one, you agree that you will not hold David Thompson, our affiliates and employees liable for any damages you may experience or incur.

Everyone's success depends on his or her background, dedication, desire, and motivation.

A Warning:

This is very powerful material. When worked properly, you may see unexpected results. These rituals and petitions are like electricity, the energy will flow in the direction of the intended output. In saying this, please be firm in your intentions and make sure what you want is truly want you desire.

As they say, be careful what you wish for, you just might get it.

To Lucifer, for this book is a pact with his greatness, and this is my offering to him for his help.

“Yahweh: You've been unhappy because you've desired things that cannot be.

Lucifer: That's what desire IS. The need for what we can't have. The need for what's readily available is called greed.”

— Mike Carey, Lucifer, Vol. 11: Evensong

I'M NOT WHO YOU THINK I AM

A short story

Observe: In a small, dimly lit chamber nestled within the confines of his ancestral home, a neophyte magician embarked on a journey that would forever alter the course of his magikal pursuits. Percival, or Percy to his friends, is the current occupant of the old house. His pudgy form was busy preparing for the ritual of all rituals. The room was adorned with ancient tomes, their leather-bound covers bearing witness to the countless hours he had spent peering into the secrets of the occult. As the candles flickered and the air grew heavy with the scent of incense, he prepared to summon a celestial being of great renown – the Dark Prince, Lucifer.

With trembling hands, he meticulously traced the intricate patterns of the summoning circle, using salt to create the protective barrier that would separate the realms of the mundane and the arcane. White chalk traced the outline of a pentagram, with strange occult symbols carefully drawn in every available spot in the circle and pentagram.

He stood back and observed the result. He sighed. It'd have to do, he'd already drawn, then erased, the summoning circle several times and was almost out of salt. Well, he mused, circles are hard! It would have helped if he'd not forgotten where he'd put the ball of twine.

The room seemed to pulse with an otherworldly energy as he recited the words of invocation, each syllable carrying the weight of centuries of magikal knowledge.

With every word he chanted, the chamber became engulfed in a profound stillness, intensifying the moment of summoning. There was a sense of suspense in the air, as if even the very molecules were holding their breath, and the room itself seemed to pulsate with excitement. Suddenly, as if a curtain had been pulled back, a presence materialized right in front of him, leaving him in awe.

It was not the figure he had expected; the horned and fearsome visage of Lucifer that had been depicted in the grimoires he had studied. Instead, before him stood a being of radiant beauty and wisdom. Wings of pure light stretched outwards from his form, casting a soft, ethereal glow that bathed the room in a gentle luminescence.

Percy could hardly believe his eyes. He blinked, then looked at the roughly drawn sigil. This was not the Lucifer of fear and darkness that he had read about in the ancient texts; this was Lucifer alright, but not the being he'd expected. Not at all. He examined the sigil again, maybe he'd gotten it wrong. Maybe he'd failed to correctly pronounce the tongue-twisting words in the ancient summoning.

With a voice that resonated like the harmonious notes of a celestial symphony, Lucifer Lightbringer addressed Percy. "Greetings, seeker of truths," he began, his eyes holding the depths of the cosmos. "You have summoned me, I am Lucifer, yes, but not the one you expected? I sense questions. What questions burn in your heart that you have called upon me this night?"

Despite himself, the sorcerer's initial surprise giving way to curiosity and he found himself compelled to ask, "Who are you, so-called Lightbringer, and what is your purpose in the grand tapestry of existence?"

Lucifer smiled gently, his radiant presence filling the room with an aura of divine serenity. "I am the one who descended to Earth not in rebellion, but out of a profound love for humanity. In the annals of cosmic history, I saw a world veiled in darkness, burdened by the weight of dogma and oppressive beliefs. It was then that I made a choice – a choice to be the beacon of enlightenment, to kindle the flames of knowledge, and to guide humanity toward the path of liberation."

And with those words, Lucifer began to weave a tale that transcended time and space. He spoke of an era when the celestial spheres spun their cosmic dance, and he observed the struggles of humankind from his vantage point among the stars. Humanity, he saw, was bound by the chains of ignorance, ensnared in the web of oppressive religious doctrines. The light of their potential was dimmed by the shadows of fear and submission.

"As I gazed upon this earthly realm," Lucifer continued, "I could not remain aloof. My heart stirred with empathy, and I knew that I must descend from the celestial realms to assist humanity in their quest for freedom and enlightenment. And so, I cast aside the trappings of divinity and descended as a guiding star, a symbol of hope and knowledge."

Percy listened intently, his mind racing with the implications of Lucifer Lightbringer's story. Here was a celestial being who had chosen to illuminate the path of humanity, even at great personal cost. It was a tale of sacrifice and love, a narrative that resonated with the deepest recesses of his being.

With reverence, Percy asked, "How can I, a humble seeker of truth, contribute to the legacy of enlightenment you have set in motion, Lucifer Lightbringer?"

Lucifer's smile illuminated the room, and his words were imbued with the wisdom of ages. "By seeking knowledge and wisdom with an open heart, by challenging the boundaries of dogma and convention, and by guiding others toward the light of understanding, you too can be a beacon of illumination. Remember, the path to enlightenment is not without its trials, but it is a journey worth embarking upon."

As their encounter drew to a close, Percy felt a profound sense of gratitude and inspiration. Lucifer Lightbringer, the aspect of Lucifer often overshadowed by tales of his fall, had graced his humble abode, and his light would forever guide the neophyte's magikal journey.

And so, in the quietude of that sacred chamber, Percival continued to explore the mysteries of the cosmos, guided by the wisdom of Lucifer, the celestial being who had descended out of love for humanity, to usher in an age of enlightenment and liberation. The young magician's path was now illuminated by the radiant wings of the Lightbringer, a beacon of knowledge and hope in a world yearning for the light of understanding.

INTRODUCTION

Lord Lucifer.

Dark Lord.

Prince of Darkness.

One of the most maligned and misjudged of all spirits.

He's what you'd expect. He is most definitely NOT Satan, nor is he Beelzebub, or any of the other assigned names. He's "Old Scratch" and he's certainly not Mephistopheles.

So, who is he?

Like Lilith, Astaroth, and numerous other spirits, Lucifer embodies various facets, distinct aspects of the same spirit, often with subtle nuances that may challenge those new to magick. However, within these pages, you'll discover the means to summon Lucifer and judge for yourself.

The most familiar aspect of Lucifer is the Egregore, the one most documented and anticipated when summoning through the traditional sigil and chant known as the ENN. Yet, in addition to the Egregore, there exists Lucifer the Fallen, Lucifer the Lightbringer, Lucifer the Creator God, and finally, Lucifer the Daemonic.

Distinguishing between the Daemonic and the Fallen traits of Lucifer can be challenging, for Lucifer the Daemonic wields exceptional abilities that transcend the usual powers associated with demons, including manipulation and vengeance. In this book, my aim is to dispel the myths surrounding Lucifer and present what I've learned in the last few decades.

Regardless of the name you employ to invoke him, Lucifer undeniably possesses immense power. While he's a master of manipulation and intrigue, he also harbors the capacity for profound love and compassion towards those close to his heart. Depending on circumstances and his emotional state, his demeanor can shift between kindness and severity. Beyond his other achievements, he's renowned for his extensive knowledge of the occult and metaphysical worlds.

His power extends to the ability to create, shape, and command the elements that surround us, from fire and water to air and earth, as well as the spiritual energies that course through the universe. He can summon and control spirits and channel potent energies into tangible forms. Manipulating the minds of others is within his grasp, bending them to his will.

Despite his formidable might, Lucifer is regarded as a being of honor and loyalty. His devotion to his followers is unwavering, and he'll spare no effort in protecting them. He holds great respect for individuals he deems worthy of his attention and rewards those who pledge their allegiance. A champion of justice and vengeance, he doesn't hesitate to punish those who wrong him or his followers.

The aspect of Lucifer I've come to know most intimately is Lucifer, the Creator God. Through a personal pathworking and a private sigil, I made contact with this aspect during a challenging period when I was recovering from major surgery, confined to a rehabilitation facility, and unable to perform regular rituals. My daughter faced sudden job termination and dire financial straits, prompting me to seek Lucifer's aid.

That evening, I sensed Lucifer's presence near me once more. I implored his assistance, asking him to help my daughter swiftly secure a better job and escape her financial woes. The following morning, I awoke to a series of texts from my daughter. She had spoken to a friend from a different animal clinic job who had just become the manager of a nearby veterinary clinic and eagerly wanted to hire her.

Additionally, her side gig of caring for horses led to a generous gift of money, helping her cover rent and emerge from her financial crisis.

Lucifer, the Creator God, swiftly responded to my request, manifesting a solution within hours. My gratitude to this aspect led me to offer the class and now this book as tokens of my appreciation.

I'll go into more detail in a later chapter on how I know this aspect, and why so very few people even know of this aspect, much less how to connect and work with this version of Lucifer.

CHAPTER 1

LUCIFER'S HISTORIES

Lucifer, often portrayed as the Dark Prince, has long held a profound allure for humanity, leaving an indelible mark on various facets of our culture. From the annals of literature and mythology to the sprawling domain of popular culture, his image has undergone a captivating evolution through the ages. The enduring fascination surrounding Lucifer among practitioners of magik and scholars of the occult has piqued curiosity for generations. Within the pages of this book, my intention is to embark on a comprehensive exploration of the multifaceted facets of this enigmatic entity and to uncover the underlying reasons for his enduring magnetism.

Lucifer's storied journey commences in ancient

mythology and religious texts, where he takes on the role of a fallen angel, cast down from the heavens due to his rebellion against the divine order. This early depiction portrays him as a figure of immense beauty and charisma, one who entices humanity with the forbidden fruits of knowledge. His character resonates deeply with humanity's yearning for autonomy and spiritual illumination, rendering him an irresistible subject for seekers of occult wisdom and personal empowerment.

As we traverse the corridors of time, Lucifer's portrayal undergoes a metamorphosis within the realm of literature. Influential works such as John Milton's "Paradise Lost" contribute to shaping his image. Here, Lucifer emerges as a tragic hero, wrestling with his desires and ambitions. This nuanced portrayal taps into our fascination with complex characters navigating the blurred boundaries between good and evil, establishing Lucifer as a timeless figure in the literary canon.

In popular culture, Lucifer emerges as a charismatic and seductive character, often portrayed as a suave and charming anti-hero. From television series like "Lucifer" to graphic novels and cinematic adaptations, this representation resonates with our fascination for rebellion and the assertion of free will. Practitioners of the occult and magik are drawn to these contemporary interpretations, viewing Lucifer as a symbol of personal liberation and the pursuit of authentic desires.

Lucifer's influence extends beyond the surface, infiltrating various subcultures. Within the occult community, Lucifer stands as a symbol of enlightenment and the exploration of hidden knowledge. Magicians and practitioners find inspiration in his rebellious spirit, embracing his archetype as a means to tap into their inner reservoirs of power.

For enthusiasts of mythology, Lucifer's representation serves as a nexus connecting diverse cultural beliefs and traditions concerning light and dark deities. Delving into Lucifer's role within various mythologies reveals a deeper understanding of universal themes that revolve around the eternal struggle between light and darkness within the human psyche.

In recent years, Luciferianism has woven itself into the fabric of media and entertainment, captivating audiences and sparking curiosity among occult scholars and magik enthusiasts.

From time immemorial, the enigmatic and captivating persona of Lucifer, the Dark Prince, has ensnared the minds of artists, writers, and filmmakers alike. This fascination has yielded a diverse and enthralling spectrum of interpretations, permeating various forms of media, including books, films, television shows, and music. It has permeated our collective consciousness, igniting a thirst to inquire into the many worlds of the forbidden and the unknown.

One of the most striking manifestations of Luciferianism in popular culture is the portrayal of Lucifer as a multifaceted and charismatic character. Frequently depicted as a rebel against oppressive forces, Lucifer has become a symbol of defiance, individuality, and self-determination. This archetype has found its way into numerous literary works, such as John Milton's "Paradise Lost" and Neil Gaiman's "Sandman" series, where Lucifer emerges as a complex figure challenging preconceived notions of good and evil.

Furthermore, Lucifer's mythological roots have served as fertile ground for a plethora of narratives. Drawing inspiration from ancient texts and religious traditions, authors and filmmakers have reimagined Lucifer's role in creation, his fall from grace, and his subsequent odyssey through realms of darkness. These reinterpretations not only underscore the enduring allure of Luciferianism, but also provide a platform for philosophical contemplation on themes of rebellion, redemption, and the human condition.

Lucifer's influence transcends literature and mythology; it extends into the realm of music and visual arts. Countless songs, album covers, and music videos pay homage to Lucifer, exploring themes of temptation, enlightenment, and spiritual awakening. These artistic expressions often serve as conduits for self-expression, challenging societal norms and encouraging individuals to embark on their own journeys of self-discovery.

In our world, the world of High Magik, the name Lucifer, holds an alluring mystique that has captivated the minds of practitioners and scholars alike. This enigmatic figure has been intertwined with various interpretations throughout history, entwining myth, religion, and popular culture. To truly grasp the immense power and significance associated with this dark prince in the practice of magick, it is imperative to disentangle the multifaceted spirit of Lucifer from the popular culture persona.

LUCIFER IN LITERATURE

For most, Lucifer is primarily known through his various depictions in popular culture. Whether encountered on the small screen or in classic novels, Lucifer has taken on a multitude of personas, ranging from a celestial being of immense power to a homicide-solving character on television.

One of the most iconic literary portrayals of Lucifer comes from John Milton's epic poem, "Paradise Lost" (1667). Here, Lucifer is introduced as a charismatic and rebellious angel who leads an unsuccessful revolt against God in

Heaven, resulting in his banishment to Hell. Milton's portrayal of Lucifer has left an indelible mark on popular culture, highlighting key themes such as pride, free will, and the eternal struggle between good and evil. Lucifer's character in this narrative is intricate and multifaceted, illustrating the seductive nature of evil and the consequences of yielding to it.

Another literary portrayal hails from Dante Alighieri's epic poem, "Inferno," part of the Divine Comedy. In this work, Lucifer appears as a colossal figure encased in ice at the very heart of Hell, where he metes out punishment to traitors, including Judas Iscariot and Brutus. Dante envisions Lucifer with three faces, each adorned with a distinct color – black, red, and yellow – and six wings. Each of his mouths chews on one of history's most infamous traitors.

Johann Wolfgang von Goethe's play "Faust" offers another unique perspective. Here, Lucifer takes on the role of Mephistopheles, a devil who tempts the protagonist, Faust, into a pact. Mephistopheles represents the embodiment of evil and serves as a counterpoint to Faust's quest for knowledge and fulfillment. Throughout the play, Mephistopheles tantalizes Faust with promises of knowledge, power, and pleasure, all in exchange for his soul. The devil's ultimate objective is to corrupt Faust's soul, and in the end, he succeeds. Nevertheless, Faust's redemption demonstrates that even in the face of temptation, one can still cling to their morality. This presentation of Lucifer within a play adds an intriguing layer to his character.

Christopher Marlowe's retelling of the Faustian myth further contributes to the literary landscape. In this tragedy, Faustus strikes a deal with Lucifer, trading his soul for power and knowledge. This iteration of Lucifer emerges as a calculating and potent figure, unafraid to challenge God and forge his own path. He embodies temptation, offering Faustus a glimpse into the forbidden and a departure from the confines of conventional morality. While this Lucifer may ultimately be a villain, he remains a multifaceted character, extending to Faustus a tantalizing glimpse beyond the boundaries of good and evil.

In more contemporary times, Neil Gaiman's "Sandman" graphic novel series introduces us to Lucifer Morningstar, the ruler of Hell who decides to retire from his post and establish a nightclub in Los Angeles. This interpretation of Lucifer garnered popularity, leading to a spin-off comic series titled "Lucifer." The narrative follows Lucifer as he endeavors to find his place in a world beyond Hell.

For most people, their knowledge of Lucifer is rooted in these literary sources. Yet, it is crucial to differentiate the true, multifaceted spirit of Lucifer from the popular culture renditions. This is akin to encountering a renowned actor who bears little resemblance to their most iconic roles on screen. Therefore, it becomes imperative to distinguish between the genuine essence of Lucifer and the popularized versions.

So, we need to separate the actual, multifaceted spirit Lucifer from the popular culture Lucifer.

Channeled Histories

This section is likely to land me in some controversial hot water.

So be it. Already, some people are upset that I separate Lucifer from all those other aspects, such as Satan. To those people, I say, "You're still attached to aspects of some brand-named religions, and you need to put away such dogma."

Working with Lucifer, especially in the context of magik, has always been a topic of controversy. Many people associate Lucifer with evil, darkness, and all things negative. However, my experiences with this being have led me to believe otherwise.

In my initial explorations in connecting with Lucifer, I admittedly adhered to the generalized and often misguided identifications, linking him with Satan, among other names. My inaugural rituals of invocation seemed futile, leaving me somewhat disheartened. As I ventured deeper, I began to unravel the multifaceted personality that is Lucifer, realizing that he stands as a unique entity, separate from Satan or any other demonized labels. Regrettably, mainstream religious doctrines amalgamate these beings, steering their followers to avoid them completely, a reflexive action akin to the universal aversion to snakes. This ingrained fear inhibits individuals from appreciating the intrinsic beauty and grandeur of these entities, much like overlooking the splendor of even the most venomous snakes that, in reality, pose no danger unless provoked.

Mass media and folklore have given birth to numerous interpretations of Lucifer, yet my personal experiences have revealed him as a mighty, divine figure, bearing qualities that are scarcely mentioned in literature. The role of Lucifer as the Creator God, a revelation documented in "The Explorer Race" series, is particularly captivating. In this narrative, Lucifer emerges as a celestial spirit that collaborates closely with the true creator of our universe. My encounters resonate with this depiction, presenting Lucifer as an elevated entity who chose to immerse himself in our reality, undergoing a gradual process of condensation until he could engage with the vibrational frequencies found in our earthly domain.

This monumental transition wasn't undertaken impulsively. Spanning millions of years, it involved taking on physical incarnations in lower dimensions, a journey towards aligning his vibrational energy with human existence, specifically within the ethereal planes of the fifth dimension, a dimension we often inhabit in the intervals between incarnations. Contrary to popular belief, the genesis of our universe was not orchestrated by YHWH, who was more of a cosmic engineer, facilitating the genesis of human vessels for soul embodiment. YHWH harbored ambitions of being revered as a deity, with intentions to guide humanity through miraculous interventions. However, Lucifer, collaborating as the co-architect of a grand experiment envisioned by the supreme creator, believed in the necessity of human autonomy for the experiment to unfold successfully. This philosophical divergence marked the beginning of a rift, leading to the historic parting of ways between Lucifer and YHWH.

Human history then embarked on cycles of rise and fall, crafting mighty civilizations, only to witness their subsequent obliteration, a cycle perpetuated through millennia. Despite these repeated upheavals, humanity has reverted to idolizing divine entities, yet still bearing the responsibility of shaping their destiny. It is speculated that the influence of YHWH was manipulated to bind humans to religious servitude, facilitating control by select elites and potentially malevolent extraterrestrial entities. In contrast, Lucifer aspires to liberate humanity from religious oppression, encouraging individuals to embrace their authentic spiritual essence.

I passionately recommend the curious and the open-minded to explore the "Explorer Race" series for a comprehensive understanding of humanity's intricate roots and their connection to the Creator God Lucifer. While my narratives and insights on Lucifer may spark debates and contention, they have unquestionably propelled me towards a profound comprehension of spirituality and the cosmos' underlying truth.

Through meditation and deep contemplation, I have been able to communicate with this entity and gain new insights into the nature of reality.

One of the key lessons I have learned from Lucifer is that there is no absolute good or evil in the universe. Rather, everything exists on a spectrum, and what we perceive as good or evil is simply a matter of perspective. This has allowed me to approach spirituality with a more nuanced and open-minded perspective, and to see beyond the simplistic dichotomy of light and darkness.

Another important insight I have gained from my experiences with Lucifer is the importance of personal responsibility. Rather than placing blame on external forces for our problems, Lucifer has taught me that we are all responsible for our own lives and the choices we make. By taking ownership of our actions and working to improve ourselves, we can overcome any obstacle and achieve our goals.

Overall, my experiences with Lucifer have been challenging, but ultimately rewarding. Through these encounters, I have gained a deeper appreciation for the complexity and mystery of the universe, and a greater sense of purpose and direction in my own life.

The Magik of Lucifer

The following chapters in this book will examine the various aspects of Lucifer I have encountered through the decades of working with Lucifer's divine light and power. Then we'll look at four unique aspects of Lucifer, any one of which you might already be familiar with, or they all may be different from any of your encounters.

With each aspect, I'll try to uncover any histories of that aspect I haven't already explored, and then I'll present specific magik rituals designed to summon that particular aspect of Lucifer. When you go to summon Lucifer the Lightbringer, light will flood your ritual space, and Lucifer Morningstar will be present. Summon Lucifer, the Creator God, and you will have a creator god in your presence. Summon Lucifer the Daemonic, that aspect of Lucifer will show up, so you'd better be ready. That petition statement had better be good and perfect, no loopholes, because Lucifer the Daemonic is a powerful daemon, and possesses the traits many magicians have a hard time figuring out and controlling.

Let me be clear, you do not control the Daemonic aspect of Lucifer. You work with this aspect, but only if this aspect knows you are worthy of his help.

Do your best to work the rituals as offered, but also consider these as just templates, to be modified for your situation, to be reworked, expanded, or simplified. In most cases, I'll present a ritual template, the details are left up to you. Choose your own candle colors, select your favorite incenses, make the offerings as suggested, and later, in ritual, ask Lucifer what he'd prefer.

Finally, get to know these different aspects of Lucifer. You'll be much wiser, confident, and your magik will vastly improve.

Pathworkings

In these pathworkings, I've endeavored to simplify the intricate process of connecting with the multifaceted aspects of Lucifer, guiding you on a journey that transcends our physical reality and immerses you in the boundless worlds where these powerful spirits reside. By following these pathworkings, you'll discover a profound shift in your approach to magik, one that liberates you from the constraints of physical rituals and allows the potent forces of magik to begin their work as soon as your mind conjures the vivid imagery.

Much like any magik ritual, it's crucial to embark on this path with careful preparation. The foundational step lies in crafting a petition statement, a potent declaration of your desires and intentions. This statement, resonating with the energy of your aspirations, serves as the key that unlocks the gates to Lucifer's presence. As you proceed, this petition statement will transform into a sigil, a symbolic representation of your deepest desires and a conduit for your connection with Lucifer's essence.

But the power of manifestation goes beyond mere words and symbols. You'll be invited to visualize your desires, to give them form and substance within the theater of your mind. This visualization becomes a living, breathing entity in the spiritual realm, a beacon that calls to the various aspects of Lucifer.

Throughout each pathworking, you'll have a unique opportunity to present your petition to Lucifer. Though you must remember that Lucifer, in his omniscience, is already attuned to the whispers of your heart and the fervor of your intentions from the very inception of your pathworking. Nevertheless, he expects you to take an active role in the process, to voice your desires with intention and sincerity. It is through this act of seeking that the wheels of manifestation are set into motion.

Imagine your petition as a sacred dialogue with these

enigmatic aspects of Lucifer. As you articulate your desires, visualize them being acknowledged and accepted by the luminous presence before you. This interaction forms a profound connection, one that bridges the gap between your earthly existence and the vast mystical places inhabited by these aspects of Lucifer.

As you undertake these pathworkings, you'll embark on a transformative journey, one that transcends the boundaries of the physical world and plunges you into the depths of spiritual exploration. The power of magik, harnessed through your connection with Lucifer, becomes a dynamic force that can reshape your reality. It's a journey that invites you to tap into the boundless potential of your own consciousness and to unlock the secrets of manifestation.

With each step you take on this path, remember that you are embarking on a voyage of profound self-discovery and spiritual awakening. The aspects of Lucifer await your presence, ready to guide and empower you on your magikal journey. Embrace the transformation, for as you do, you'll find that the lines between the physical and nonphysical worlds blur, and the realm of possibility stretch far beyond your previous imaginings.

Defining Your Desire

Prior to embarking on the journey of magik rituals and invoking any specific aspect, it is important to have a clear vision of what you seek to achieve. We must begin with the foundational step of defining our desire. This is the moment when we drill down to the very essence of what we seek to manifest in our lives. Picture it as excavating for a hidden treasure within the depths of your consciousness. Just as an archaeologist carefully brushes away layers of earth to reveal an ancient artifact, we must gently peel back the layers of our desires to uncover their true core.

Think of a desire as a multifaceted gem, each facet representing a layer of complexity. For instance, you might desire wealth, but that's just the surface. Why do you want wealth? Is it for financial security, the ability to travel, or perhaps the freedom to pursue your passions without worry? By asking these questions, you begin to chip away at the layers, revealing the glittering core of your desire.

Consider the analogy of a beautiful rose. At first glance, you're captivated by its vibrant petals, but it's the fragrance, the delicate interplay of colors, and the softness of its touch that make it truly enchanting. Similarly, your desire may appear simple on the surface, but its true beauty lies in the nuances, the underlying reasons that make it meaningful to you.

In magik, we are not interested in superficial wants; we aim to unearth the profound desires that resonate with the very essence of our being. It's akin to deciphering a cryptic message encoded within your soul. Only by peeling back the layers can you truly understand what you're seeking to manifest.

Crafting the Magik Petition: Words that Ignite the Flame

Once we've excavated our desires and reached their core, the next step is to put them into words. Crafting a magik petition is an art form in itself, a sacred act of transforming the intangible into the tangible. It's akin to taking the raw materials of your desire and forging them into a powerful incantation that can bridge the sphere of the physical and the metaphysical.

Imagine you're an alchemist in a hidden laboratory, surrounded by ancient tomes and mystical ingredients. Your task is to distill the essence of your desire into a potion that will spark the flames of manifestation. Each word you choose is like a mystical ingredient, contributing to the potency of your magik.

The key here is precision. Your words must be clear and concise, leaving no room for ambiguity. Think of them as the navigational coordinates guiding the energy of your desire to its destination. Just as a ship needs accurate charts to reach its port, your magik petition requires exact words to manifest your desires.

Consider the following analogy: You are an artist

painting a masterpiece. Each brushstroke must be deliberate and purposeful. Every stroke adds depth and detail, just as each word in your petition imbues it with power and intention. It's the difference between a vague request and a command that the universe cannot ignore.

Removing Unnecessary Restrictions: Setting Your Desire Free

As we continue our magikal journey, it's essential to remove any unnecessary restrictions that may inhibit the flow of energy toward your desire. Imagine your desire as a river, and restrictions as boulders obstructing its path. By clearing away these impediments, you allow the river of manifestation to flow freely and powerfully.

Think of restrictions as self-imposed limitations or doubts that may creep into your mind. They can take the form of thoughts like "I'm not worthy of this" or "It's impossible." These mental barriers are like chains that bind your desire, preventing it from soaring to its full potential.

Imagine you're a sculptor working on a masterpiece. Your desire is the raw material, and these restrictions are the excess stone that needs to be chiseled away. As you chip away the doubts and fears, you reveal the exquisite form of your desire beneath.

In magik, we understand that the universe operates on

the principle of abundance. There are no limitations to what can be manifested, except those we place upon ourselves. By removing these self-imposed restrictions, you open the floodgates to infinite possibilities. It's like unlocking a treasure chest filled with boundless riches of the universe.

The only exception to this rule applies specifically when you are working with the Daemonic aspect of Lucifer or the daemonic aspect of any being. In such cases, it is crucial to emphasize that you do not wish for your desire to manifest at the expense of anyone's well-being, including instances like receiving an inheritance from a beloved grandparent. The best practice is to simply add: "Manifest my desire harming none." That simple.

Transforming Your Desire into a Sigil: The Art of Symbolism

Once your magik petition is honed to perfection, the next step is to transform it into a sigil. A sigil is a symbol imbued with the essence of your desire, a visual representation of your intention. Think of it as a mystical beacon that calls out to the universe, broadcasting your desire with laser-like precision.

Creating a sigil is like forging a mystical talisman that encapsulates your magikal intent. It condenses the power of your words into a single, potent symbol that bypasses the conscious mind and directly communicates with the subconscious and the spiritual realms.

Imagine you're a blacksmith, fashioning a sword that carries the power to cut through the veil of reality. Each curve and line etched into the blade represents an aspect of your desire, and when wielded correctly, it becomes an instrument of transformation.

A well-crafted sigil is like a key that unlocks the door to manifestation. It's a symbol that speaks the language of the universe, a universal code that transcends barriers and resonates with the energetic currents of creation.

I have a free course in crafting a sigil, found on my e-learning website, link in the appendix.

CHAPTER 2

THE LIGHTBRINGER

While working with Lucifer, I have become familiar with multiple aspects. Each one presents an amazingly complex spirit. Since the Lightbringer is a bit more familiar with people who practice High Magik, I'll start with this aspect.

I'm going to examine the intricacies of this aspect, from the very beginning of currently accepted mythology and lore, and then we'll go into the more maleficent shadows of Lucifer.

The story of Lucifer, a name that has echoed throughout history, begins in distant places that are far removed from the common perception of evil that modern interpretations often associate with him. Lucifer, a figure steeped in rich historical and metaphorical tapestry, represents a journey from the bringer of dawn to an emblem of rebellion and individualism. It is this transition, replete with layers of meaning and perspectives, that we inquire into in this section.

The name "Lucifer" finds its origin in the Latin vernacular, a beautiful amalgamation of "lux" (light) and "ferre" (to bring), thereby etymologically translating to "light-bringer" or "morning star". This appellation is often ascribed to the planet Venus, known for its bright, dawn-like appearance in the sky before sunrise. In early Roman poetry and myth, Lucifer was perceived as a herald of dawn, a beacon that signaled the advent of a new day, dispelling the darkness that engulfed the world.

To grasp the multifaceted nature of Lucifer, it is necessary to traverse back to the ancient texts that form the bedrock of his characterization. In the ancient Canaanite religion, a deity akin to Lucifer was known as Helel, a figure associated with the morning star, representing light and brilliance. This deity embarks on a journey that mirrors that of the eventual Christian interpretation of Lucifer, one of a rise and subsequent fall.

As time progressed, the figure of Lucifer began to undergo a metamorphosis, notably in the Judeo-Christian traditions. In the Christian Bible, particularly in the book of

Isaiah, we encounter a shift where Lucifer comes to be depicted as a fallen angel, cast down from the heavenly realms due to an act of rebellion. I'll pick up the "Fallen" aspect in a few chapters.

To navigate the rich tapestry of symbolism encompassing Lucifer the Lightbringer, it is incumbent upon us to transcend the binary narratives that have dominated his discourse. As we venture deeper into the layers of symbolism associated with the Lightbringer, we unearth a complex panorama that transcends traditional dichotomies, unveiling a figure that embodies both enlightenment and shadow, rebellion and wisdom. In this section, we venture through the labyrinthine corridors of symbolism, exploring the intricate web of meanings that Lucifer, in his Lightbringer facet, unfurls.

THE HARBINGER OF DAWN

In the early morn, during those precious moments where night softly gives way to day, the celestial canvas hosts a resplendent entity, the morning star, synonymous with Lucifer. Its luminous presence in the sky, even before the first rays of the sun tenderly grace the earth, stands as a potent and enduring symbol in the intricate narratives woven around the figure of Lucifer the Lightbringer.

This spectacle of the morning star shining bright

amidst the pre-dawn sky carries a multitude of profound symbologies, painting a canvas rich with layers of meaning and depth. Foremost, it embodies hope, a luminous beacon piercing through the engulfing darkness that pervades the land before the dawn. Its light, steadfast and serene, becomes a sentinel in the night, a glowing testament to the persistent flicker of hope that dances even in the densest hours of darkness. It serves as a gentle reminder that no matter the depth of the night's darkness, a guiding force, a beacon of light, is always present, ready to shepherd us towards the promising embrace of a new dawn, fostering fresh realizations and igniting sparks of renewed vigor and life.

Furthermore, the morning star heralds a time of renewal, a cyclical dance of beginnings that resonates deeply with the rhythms of the natural world. Its appearance in the sky serves as a celestial cue, marking the end of one cycle and the beginning of another, reminding us of the inexhaustible flow of time that carries within it the promise of rebirth and rejuvenation. In the silent whispers exchanged between the morning star and the approaching dawn, we find narratives of hope, a poetic dialogue that fosters a resilient spirit, encouraging us to embrace the potential of what lies ahead with open hearts and eager souls.

As I inquired deeper, tracing the intricate arc of Lucifer's narrative through the annals of history, I encountered manifestations of his more familiar revolutionary aspect, an embodiment of fiery rebellion and fierce individualism. In this role, Lucifer transcends the boundaries of mere folklore to stand as a robust emblem of defiance against established norms and unquestioned traditions. This facet of Lucifer embodies the raw, untamed courage to challenge the status quo, to scrutinize the dictums handed down through generations with a discerning eye and a questioning spirit.

Lucifer, in this revolutionary persona, becomes a catalyst for personal evolution and growth, encouraging individuals to break free from the suffocating chains of conformity that bind the spirit and dampen the luminous flame of individuality. He emerges as a force that fervently champions the quest for personal truth and autonomy, urging us to carve paths that resonate with our inner compass, paths adorned with the essence of our unique selves.

In his call for rebellion, there is an invitation to embark upon a journey of self-discovery, an exploration of the deeper worlds of the self that remain obscured in the shadows of societal expectations and imposed norms. Lucifer beckons us to foster a vibrant spirit of inquiry, to cultivate a garden where questions bloom in profusion, fostering a climate where personal truths can emerge unswayed by the imposing structures of established thought.

Through the ages, Lucifer has stood as a mirror reflecting the intrinsic human desire for freedom, for the space to express one's truest self without the burden of judgment or the weight of expectations. He encourages a journey steeped in personal autonomy, where the individual becomes the master of their destiny, forging paths that resonate with authenticity and integrity.

In this nuanced narrative that intertwines the celestial symbolism of the morning star with the fiery spirit of rebellion, we find a rich tapestry that invites exploration and reflection. It is a narrative that encourages us to embrace the luminous potential within, urging us to step into the light of a new dawn, fortified with the wisdom gleaned from introspective journeys and the courage to stand as sovereign beings in a world in perpetual flux.

THE PURSUER OF KNOWLEDGE

Another powerful symbol associated with the Lightbringer is the relentless pursuit of knowledge. In various narratives, Lucifer emerges as a figure hungry for wisdom and enlightenment, a being not content with the boundaries placed upon him. This aspect encourages practitioners of magik to continually seek knowledge, to inquire deeper into the mysteries of existence, urging them to never be complacent, but to continually aspire to higher levels of understanding and wisdom.

He is often thought of as the serpent who tempted Eve with the fruit of the Tree of Knowledge while in the Garden. This association with knowledge is also seen in the mythological figure of Prometheus, who stole fire from the gods and gave it to humanity, symbolizing the gift of knowledge and enlightenment. The pursuit of knowledge is therefore seen as a rebellious act, challenging the established order and seeking to transcend limitations.

In many spiritual traditions, the pursuit of knowledge is seen as a path towards spiritual enlightenment, as it allows individuals to gain greater insight into the nature of reality and the workings of the universe. This is why many practitioners of magik place a strong emphasis on studying various esoteric and occult disciplines, including astrology, numerology, alchemy, and divination.

Ultimately, the pursuit of knowledge is seen as a way of connecting with the divine and accessing higher levels of consciousness. By continually seeking wisdom and understanding, practitioners of magik hope to unlock the secrets of the universe and tap into the infinite power of the Lightbringer.

THE BRINGER OF LIGHT AND ENLIGHTENMENT

Central to the persona of Lucifer the Lightbringer is

his monumental role as a beacon of enlightenment, a luminary figure who holds the lantern high in the world of shadows, illuminating pathways veiled in obscurity and nurturing seeds of wisdom in the hearts of seekers. Throughout the annals of time, Lucifer has transformed, metamorphosing into a potent symbol of enlightenment that transcends conventional boundaries, offering guidance and light where confusion and darkness prevail.

In his role as a beacon of enlightenment, Lucifer emerges as a force that beckons individuals to peer beyond the superficial, to dive deeper into the complexities of existence, unraveling truths that lie shrouded in mystery. He encourages us to transcend the mundane realities of existence, to eschew the trivialities that often cloud our judgment and perception, urging us to reach for realms that resonate with profound wisdom and understanding.

This facet of Lucifer serves as a pillar, supporting those on a journey to explore the unknown corners of their being, guiding them through the winding paths of personal growth and spiritual evolution. He embodies the spirit of the vigilant guide, one who stands steadfast, illuminating the rocky terrains of the spiritual journey, offering respite and clarity amidst the swirling vortex of confusion that often engulfs those treading the path less traveled.

In the complex, multifaceted spheres of magik, this

luminous aspect of Lucifer comes forth as a guiding force, a mentor who assists practitioners in navigating the intricate corridors of the mystical journey. His energy permeates the sacred spaces where magik unfolds, weaving a tapestry of light that helps decipher the codes of ancient wisdom, unveiling secrets that foster growth and enlightenment.

Within the intricate dance of shadows and light, practitioners find in Lucifer a dependable ally, one who holds the torch high, casting a glow that pierces through the veil of ignorance, revealing pathways adorned with profound knowledge and insight. His presence becomes a sanctuary, a haven of light where seekers can find solace, rejuvenate their spirits, and garner strength to continue their journey with renewed vigor and clarity.

In times of confusion, when the labyrinthine twists and turns of life engulf the practitioner, Lucifer's role as a beacon of enlightenment becomes a vital force, a compass that helps realign with the true North of personal truth and integrity. He encourages individuals to cultivate a discerning eye, to sift through the noise and chaos, guiding them towards a sanctuary of wisdom where truth resonates with crystal clear clarity.

Moreover, Lucifer the Lightbringer emerges as a transformative force, a catalyst that ignites the flame of awareness, fostering a deep-seated understanding and connection with the cosmos and the intricate web of energies that permeate it. He beckons us to embrace our roles as luminous beings, capable of transcending the limitations imposed by the physical world, urging us to reach for the stars, to aspire for a state of being that resonates with light, wisdom, and universal harmony.

Thus, central to Lucifer's persona is an invitation to embark on a journey of enlightenment, a voyage that promises growth, evolution, and the unveiling of truths that have the potential to liberate the soul, fostering a state of existence that is luminous, enlightened, and harmoniously connected with the intricate dance of the cosmos.

THE GUARDIAN OF INDIVIDUALISM

In the figure of the Lightbringer, a kaleidoscope of profound qualities coalesce, presenting us with a staunch guardian of individualism, a celestial entity that fervently champions the sacred cause of personal freedom and self-determination. The narrative woven around Lucifer is not just an account of rebellion and enlightenment, but a compelling saga that encourages individuals to unfurl their true selves, unapologetically and with utmost valor, in a world that often seeks conformity and uniformity.

Embarking upon a closer examination of Lucifer's role as a protector of individuality, we witness a figure radiant with the iridescent glow of personal freedom, a beacon that illuminates paths leading towards autonomy and personal mastery. Through his narrative, a profound lesson unfolds, teaching us the virtues of embracing our unique selves, urging us to carve out niches where our true essence can flourish uninhibited, unswayed by the clamoring voices of the masses that often drown the whispers of the individual spirit.

In the grand tapestry of existence, Lucifer stands as a reminder of the singular journey each one is on. He beckons us to listen intently to the nuanced symphonies of our souls, to dance to rhythms that resonate with our innermost beings, fostering a sanctuary where the unique attributes of each individual are celebrated and nurtured. It is here, in this sanctified space, that the seeds of original thoughts, ideas, and perspectives are sown, cultivated with the nourishing waters of personal insight and experience.

Lucifer's urging to cultivate a strong sense of individuality is not a mere call to dissent but a profound invitation to explore the depths of one's being, to forge connections with the inner worlds where the true essence resides. This journey within is a vital aspect in the practice of magik, where the practitioner is encouraged to forge a path adorned with personal experiences and revelations, weaving a rich tapestry that holds the key to unlocking potent energies and pathways in the mystical spheres.

The world of magik is not one of monochrome hues, but a vibrant cosmos pulsating with a plethora of experiences, energies, and phenomena. It is a reality where personal insights are not just valued but hold a significant position in crafting potent spells, invoking energies, and navigating the labyrinthine corridors of the mystical world. In this domain, Lucifer emerges as a guiding force, nurturing the practitioner's journey, fostering an environment where personal narratives are woven into the grander tapestry of mystical practices, enriching it with depth, perspective and nuance.

Furthermore, embracing individuality under Lucifer's guardianship transcends mere personal growth, morphing into a potent catalyst for community development and societal progression. When individuals are encouraged to hone their unique perspectives and strengths, it fosters a society vibrant with diversity, innovation, and creativity, a community that is reflective of the myriad hues of human experience and existence.

Therefore, in the narrative of the Lightbringer, we find an urgent call to protect and nurture the sanctity of individualism, to foster spaces where personal freedom and self-determination are not mere concepts but living realities, breathing life into the practice of magik, and fostering a world where the luminous glow of individuality lights up the cosmos with its vibrant, unique, and irreplaceable sparkle.

THE CATALYST OF TRANSFORMATION

In the complex and vibrant tableau of spiritual narratives, Lucifer, in his esteemed Lightbringer aspect, unfurls as a potent catalyst for deep and lasting transformation, a dynamic entity pulsating with energies that fervently drive change, growth, and evolution on both personal and cosmic scales.

At the very essence of his being, Lucifer harbors energies that are in a perpetual state of flux, vibrant forces that channel the raw, untamed powers of transformation. This transcendent force, an elemental energy that courses through the veins of the cosmos, finds a passionate advocate in the figure of the Lightbringer. He stands as a beacon, an epicenter of seismic shifts that beckon individuals to inquire into the crucible of change, to immerse themselves fully in the potent currents of growth and evolution that swirl in the celestial realms he governs.

With a guiding hand, extended in both solace and challenge, Lucifer invites seekers to embark on transformative journeys, quests that are as exhilarating as they are demanding. These journeys are not for the faint of heart; they require a fervent courage, a willingness to traverse uncharted territories, to peer into the abyss and find not fear, but potential. It is through his guidance, a wisdom wrought from the fiery forges of rebellion and enlightenment, that individuals find the fortitude to shed old skins, to cast aside the worn-out mantles of past selves that no longer serve their evolving narratives.

In the nurturing embrace of the Lightbringer, individuals find a sanctuary where they can undergo metamorphosis, a sacred space where the chrysalis of the old self can dissolve, giving way to a renewed, enlightened, and empowered being. This process of transformation, under Lucifer's watchful eye, is a dance of both destruction and creation, a delicate ballet where the old gives way to the new, where decay fosters growth, and where endings herald beginnings. It is a cyclical process, a rhythm that beats at the heart of existence, a pulse that nourishes the ever-evolving tapestry of life.

But Lucifer's role extends beyond mere guidance; he actively nurtures the flame of inner transformation, fostering an environment where seekers can flourish in their newfound strength and wisdom. His energy infuses the practitioner with a luminous fire, a blaze that ignites the inner sanctum of the soul, awakening dormant potentials and kindling the sparks of divine insight and inspiration. Through this fiery baptism, individuals emerge not just renewed, but reborn, carrying within them the luminous seeds of newfound perspectives, heightened awareness, and a vibrant, pulsating connection to the cosmos and its intricate web of energies and forces.

Under the guardianship of Lucifer the Lightbringer, individuals are not merely transformed; they are elevated, lifted to levels where they can perceive the luminous threads that weave the complex fabric of existence. Here, in this enlightened state, they stand empowered, ready to step into their roles as architects of their destinies, as masters of their evolving narratives, carrying within them the radiant glow of enlightenment, a luminous beacon in a cosmos vibrant with the dance of ceaseless change and growth.

POWERS OF LUCIFER

Lucifer, especially the Lightbringer aspect, has unique traits when it comes to using this aspect in magik. I have split this into two sections - internal transformation using Lucifer, and more practical aspects of this magik, such as wealth, family, and business. These powers can be asked of any Lucifer aspect, not just the Lightbringer aspect.

Internal Transformation

1. **Spiritual Enlightenment**: Utilize the Lightbringer's energy to shed light on spiritual mysteries and uncover deeper truths that lie within the self, propelling towards a path of wisdom and understanding.
2. **Personal Transformation**: Leverage Lucifer's

energies as a catalyst for profound personal transformation, helping in the shedding of old, unhelpful patterns and fostering growth and evolution.

3. **Healing and Restoration**: Drawing upon the rejuvenating energies of the morning star to facilitate healing and restoration, both on a personal and communal level.

4. **Illumination of Shadows**: Employ the light of Lucifer to illuminate the shadows within the self, helping to integrate and transform these aspects, fostering a balanced and harmonized being.

5. **Enhancing Creativity**: Utilizing Lucifer's energies to ignite a creative spark, encouraging the expression of one's unique perspective and fostering innovation and originality in various artistic pursuits.

6. **Empowerment and Autonomy**: Drawing upon the energies of Lucifer to foster empowerment and autonomy, encouraging individuals to carve their path, defined by personal truth and sovereignty.

7. **Mastering Challenges**: Utilize the courage and rebellious energy of Lucifer to overcome challenges and adversities, fostering resilience and determination.

8. **Guidance in Magikal Practices**: Seeking guidance from Lucifer in magikal practices, using his wisdom and insight to enhance one's skill and understanding in the occult arts.

9. **Divination and Clairvoyance**: Using the energies of the Lightbringer to enhance abilities in divination and clairvoyance, providing clearer insights and foresights in various forms of divinatory practices.

10. **Sacred Knowledge and Learning**: Drawing upon Lucifer's association with knowledge to facilitate learning and mastery in various fields of study, fostering a deep understanding and proficiency in chosen subjects.

Deep Exploration of the Self

Initiating this journey requires a deep and honest exploration of oneself. It involves peeling away layers of societal conditioning and ego-driven perspectives to reveal the core essence of one's being. Utilizing the Lightbringer's energy here works as a potent catalyst, illuminating the dark corners of the self, uncovering hidden fears, desires, and potentials that reside within. It invites an individual to inquire deep into their psyche, to encounter and understand the primal forces and energies that drive them.

Unveiling Spiritual Mysteries

Beyond the self, this energy can also aid in unveiling the larger spiritual mysteries of existence. It encourages a seeker to ponder the profound questions of life, death, and the cosmos. Through this process, individuals may find themselves developing a deeper connection with the universe, understanding the intricate web of connections that bind all things. The Lightbringer serves as a guide, offering illumination in the exploration of esoteric knowledge, ancient philosophies, and spiritual doctrines that provide insight into the nature of reality and existence.

Path of Wisdom and Understanding

As one progresses on this path, they cultivate a wisdom that transcends mundane understanding. This wisdom is characterized by a profound appreciation for the complexity and beauty of existence. It fosters a deep-seated understanding that enables individuals to navigate the complexities of life with grace and insight.

Furthermore, the journey with the Lightbringer's energy nurtures a capacity for empathy and compassion, as the understanding of oneself expands to encompass an understanding of others. It fosters a harmonious relationship with the surroundings, encouraging individuals to act as beacons of light themselves, propagating wisdom and understanding in their communities.

ENHANCED MAGIKAL PROFICIENCY

For practitioners adept in magik, like yourself, utilizing the energies of the Lightbringer can significantly enhance magikal proficiency. It can aid in developing a more profound understanding of magikal theories and enhance the ability to manipulate energies and forces during rituals and workings. It's a pathway to mastering higher levels of magik, encompassing an understanding that integrates both light and shadow aspects, leading to a balanced and potent practice.

Integration and Transformation

This journey is one of continuous integration and transformation. It demands a commitment to personal growth, a willingness to shed outdated perspectives, and embrace new, enlightened viewpoints. It's a transformative process that molds an individual into a being of higher consciousness, a being who embodies wisdom, understanding, and light - mirroring the qualities of the Lightbringer himself.

Engaging with Lucifer in this aspect is not merely a process of seeking external guidance, but a transformative journey where an individual is shaped and refined by the potent energies of the Lightbringer, emerging as a beacon of light in their right.

MONEY AND WEALTH MAGIK:

1. **Wealth Attraction and Manifestation**: Using the energies to illuminate opportunities and pathways for

wealth attraction, helping to manifest abundance in material aspects.

2. **Financial Wisdom**: Seeking guidance from Lucifer to develop a deeper understanding and wisdom in handling financial matters adeptly, fostering wealth preservation and growth.

3. **Prosperity Rituals**: Incorporating his energies in rituals aimed at enhancing prosperity, potentially bringing forth luck and fortune in financial endeavors.

FAMILY MAGIK:

1. **Harmony and Unity**: Drawing upon his energies to foster harmony and unity within the family, helping to resolve conflicts and enhance mutual understanding and cooperation.

2. **Protection**: Using his energies as a shield to protect the family from negative influences and energies, safeguarding the home and the loved ones.

3. **Spiritual Growth**: Encouraging family members to embark on their spiritual journeys, fostering growth and enlightenment within the family unit, and creating a

spiritually nurturing environment.

LOVE AND ROMANCE MAGIK:

1. **Attraction and Passion**: Leveraging his energies to ignite the flames of attraction and passion, helping to foster romantic relationships characterized by depth and intensity.

2. **Healing Broken Relationships**: Using the light-bringing aspect to heal broken relationships, helping to mend wounds and foster reconciliation.

3. **Self-Love**: Employing his energies to foster self-love, encouraging individuals to recognize and appreciate their worth, thereby attracting relationships that mirror this appreciation.

BUSINESS MAGIK:

1. **Insight and Innovation**: Drawing upon Lucifer's energies to foster insight and innovation in business, helping to identify opportunities for growth and expansion.

2. **Leadership and Charisma**: Utilizing his energies to enhance leadership qualities and charisma, fostering a

strong and influential position in the business domain.

3. **Protection Against Business Rivalries**: Using his energies for protection against business rivalries and negative energies aimed at destabilizing the business.

4. **Contracts and Agreements**: Seeking guidance in matters of contracts and agreements, ensuring favorable terms and successful business partnerships.

RITUAL PREPARATIONS

Preparing for a ritual to Lucifer the Lightbringer is similar to preparing for any ritual to any deity. Make sure you know what you want, have a prepared petition ready.

Entire books have been written about formulating your desire as a petition to a deity, so I'll be brief. Keep the statement simple, using phrases such as "I desire…" and "Assist me in manifesting…" always worked best. I prefer to work very simple petitions. The more conditions you put in a petition, the greater the chance the magik fails. I prefer to put in a goal, then add "swiftly". The spirits you summon for any magik are there to assist you in manifesting your desire. They add their own power to yours, raising your energy levels such that the universe has no choice but to deliver your desire. Yes, we can work magik minus any rituals and summonings, just our own mental powers applied to the goal, will cause the desire to manifest. But it's so much easier with the power of a spirit.

Another key element in any ritual preparation is to practice visualizing. Our minds are funny in that if we do a good enough job in visualizing the outcome, our powerful minds will adjust and rearrange our reality to make your vision happen.

Remember to approach this ritual (and others) with sincerity and a genuine desire for enlightenment and growth.

For this aspect of Lucifer, we'll need some specific items to offer, plus specific candles that resonate with this aspect. The Lightbringer needs white candles to represent the pure light of Lucifer. Incense should be frankincense and myrrh. It's preferable to use resin and a piece of incense charcoal, and not those overly perfumed incense sticks.

When it comes to this aspect, it is important to limit the offerings to libations such as a good wine or spirits like whiskey or vodka. As traditional for a ritual, the offering is left on Lucifer's sigil overnight, then poured out onto the ground the next day. You can also give cake or a valuable herb, like saffron. In such offerings, dispose of these into nature the next day.

Another good offering for this aspect of Lucifer is to go out and "do good works." A bit on the vague side, I admit, but this is what the aspect said to me. So, I inquired further, and got to volunteer helping a kitchen feed the homeless, and not just at Thanksgiving (US Holiday) or Christmas, but on a random Saturday or middle of the week, when such facilities really need the help.

However, unless you're volunteering at a new age led charity, it's a good idea to keep the purpose of the volunteering to yourself. Make up a misdirection to account for your presence. Especially in the US south, where religion tends to dominate such facilities. They won't really understand.

RITUAL TO LUCIFER THE LIGHTBRINGER

This basic ritual to Lucifer Lightbringer is as simple as I can make it and remains quite effective. Think of it as a template, and just alter to fit your needs.

As we are working with a powerful spirit, you do not need to concern yourself with astronomical alignments, and work the ritual when the time is best for you. Many of the items suggested are just that: suggestions. Non-optional items are marked at an (*)

Items needed:

- A white or gold candle to represent the Lightbringer's illuminating aspects.*
- Ritual specific candle (see appendix for color

associations)

- Incense (preferably frankincense or myrrh) to facilitate a sacred atmosphere.*
- Lucifer Lightbringer Sigil (Appendix)*
- Crystals like clear quartz or selenite to amplify the energies.
- Your petition*
- Offering and offering bowl or glass*

When ready, light the incense charcoal or stick. Then light the altar candles and save lighting the ritual candle until it's time to light it after it is blessed by Lucifer.

Cast a simple circle (appendix). Once this has been done, proceed with the summoning:

Say:

Lucifer, Bringer of Dawn, Luminary of the Morning Star,

I call upon you in your most radiant aspect,

I seek the wisdom of your illuminating light,

Come forth, O Keeper of Enlightenment,

Guide me in the path of transcendent wisdom and personal mastery.

Hail Lucifer, the Lightbringer, the morning's herald.

Pause a few moments and await the subtle shifts in the room's air that may indicate that Lucifer Lightbringer has arrived. The presence is warming; you feel at ease; you feel the warmth of his love for all humans in this aspect.

Pick up your petition and read over it. Then, read it out loud.

Once you have read your petition, pause a few moments. Visualize the intended outcome. Try to see as much detail as you can. Try to bring up the emotions associated with your desire being fulfilled.

Once you have done this, pick up the sigil you made from the petition, if you have one (if not, skip ahead to the candle). Hold this sigil in one hand, and trace over the lines with your other hand, then ask:

"Lucifer, Lightbringer, please bless and activate this sigil so that my desire may manifest in my life!"

Once this is done, pick up the candle for this desire, and hold it up. Then say:

"Lightbringer! Morningstar! I now ask that you bless this candle to bring to me my desire, so that it may manifest in my life!"

At this point, it's time for the offering. I suggest a libation of red wine. If doing good works in Lucifer's name, simply tell him what you intend to do. Otherwise, pour a small amount of the wine into the offering bowl, and set it on his sigil.

Say: **"Lucifer Lightbringer! I now humbly offer to you this wine (or whatever it is) in gratitude for acting on my petition!"**

If doing good works, say **"Lucifer Lightbringer, I will be ____________________________ in your honor, please accept this as my offering, in you name."**

The ritual is finished at this point.

You can close the ritual in any way you feel you need to close it or use my method. What I do is, I hold my hands out over the ritual sigil, candle, and Lucifer's sigil. I then imagine energy, gold, or silver, flowing through my body and into my hands, then unto the sigil, candle, or other ritual items. I'll then say something like:

"Into this sigil, into this magik candle, I direct great powers. Power drawn from Lucifer himself, and power drawn from my own higher self, to energize and enchant these symbols to achieve the manifestation of my desire!"

Hold this a few breaths. Really hit these items with this energy.

To finish the ritual, say something like "This circle

now open, but never broken!"

Snuff out the altar candles and allow the ritual candle to burn completely. Do this safely!

Wait overnight to dispose of the offering. Wine can be poured out onto the ground. Sweets can be left in nature. If doing good works, plan to try to do this within a fortnight (14 days or two weeks, etc.) from the end of the ritual.

PATHWORKING LUCIFER LIGHTBRINGER

This pathworking places you in the same energetic space as the divine aspect of Lucifer the Lightbringer.

The Journey begins

Visualization: Visualize yourself standing under the morning sky just before dawn, the Morning Star shining brightly.

Energy Attunement: Feel your energy attuning with the energy of the morning star, embracing its qualities of hope, renewal, and enlightenment.

Affirmation: Affirm your readiness to embrace the transformative energies that Lucifer, as the Lightbringer, offers.

Step Two: Encounter

Journey Deeper: As you stand under the morning

star, feel yourself being drawn towards its light, journeying deeper into its luminous realms.

Encounter with Lucifer: Encounter Lucifer in a form that resonates with his Lightbringer aspect — as a luminous being, a guardian of wisdom and enlightenment.

Dialog: Engage in a dialog with him, asking questions or seeking guidance regarding your personal journey or transformation. Present your desire or petition, asking for favor.

Receiving Light: Allow yourself to receive the Lightbringer's illuminating energies, infusing you with wisdom, courage, and insight.

Step Three: Return and Integration

Gratitude: Express your gratitude to Lucifer for the guidance and insights provided.

Return Journey: Gradually return to your physical surroundings, retracing your steps back to your initial starting point under the morning sky.

Grounding: Ground yourself by visualizing roots extending from your feet into the earth, anchoring you firmly to the physical world.

Integration: Note down your experiences in a journal. Reflect on the insights gained and consider how to integrate them into your life for personal growth and transformation.

Step Four: Offering

Run the simple gratitude ritual (appendix) and offer Lucifer a libation of wine or spirits, placing this on his sigil over night. Then dispose of the libation in nature.

CHAPTER 3

Unveiling the Concept of Lucifer as a Creator God

Here, I'll unveil a unique concept: Lucifer as a Creator God from outside our universe, a revelation that defies the boundaries of conventional wisdom and propels us into the universe of cosmic magik.

This aspect is what I call "exouniverse" in origin. "Exo" meaning from outside, and "Universe," which is our reality, the creation which came into being billions of years ago.

This is the aspect I use almost as often as the Lightbringer aspect. Along with its unique origins, this aspect exhibits unique magik which can be useful in many situations.

To wrap our head around this concept, you will have to accept the idea that our creation has a specific creator, and this creator exists outside our universe. In this concept, our creator is but one of many creator spirits who will run experiments in the universes they create. Going further, we have to open our minds to the idea of multiple creators, multiple universes/creations, varying physical properties of each creation/universe. Several creators can be working on any one creation/universe at a time. Perhaps this is part of an education lab, where creator students learn their craft?

Then, within this concept, we have a situation of a separate creator spirit joining with the creator of our reality, to run an experiment. This experiment is in dealing with a unique energy form, what we'd call "negativity".

In this concept, Lucifer is not merely a participant but the grand orchestrator of the negativity experiment, a Creator God himself whose artistry extends beyond the boundaries of our known universe. His perspective is as boundless as the cosmos itself, for he stands outside its confines, viewing the grand masterpiece of creation with an artist's eye.

Lucifer's role as a Creator God goes beyond the conventional narratives of divinity; he is not bound by the limitations of our earthly perceptions. Instead, he exists as a cosmic architect, shaping the very fabric of existence with his celestial brushstrokes.

Now, let us journey deeper into the heart of this concept, unraveling the cosmic mysteries that surround Lucifer as a Creator God. Our exploration shall lead us to the profound insights chronicled in the works of Robert Shapiro and the unique perspective and abilities that define Lucifer in this cosmic role.

His Role in an Experiment on Earth

The chronicles of Lucifer as a Creator God find their resonance in the pages of "Explorer Race," a series of books by Robert Shapiro. Within the annals of this remarkable book series, a narrative unfolds—one that challenges our understanding of Lucifer and his involvement in the affairs of Earth.

Imagine the Earth as a grand laboratory, a crucible of evolution and transformation. Within this laboratory, Lucifer assumes the role of a cosmic scientist, overseeing an experiment of profound significance. His purpose? To guide and catalyze ways to deal with negativity and to evolve the energy necessary to neutralize this negative energy.

As I read the ideas in the book, "Explorer Race," I discovered the notion that Lucifer's experiment is not driven by mere curiosity, but by a profound desire to uplift and awaken the consciousness of humanity. His intentions, shrouded in cosmic wisdom, extend beyond the boundaries of our individual lives, reaching into the tapestry of collective evolution.

Consider Lucifer as the cosmic mentor, providing humanity with the tools and challenges necessary for spiritual growth and enlightenment. Through the eons, he has acted as the guiding force behind the scenes, gently nudging humanity towards the realization of its divine potential. This was thrown into conflict with another spirit, one you might have heard of, the spirit Jehovah, or YHWH. Jehovah was tasked by the creator to organize a colony on this planet, shape it, design a vessel suitable to house human souls,

The experiment, as explained by Shapiro, reveals a perspective of Lucifer as a benevolent Creator God, whose actions are driven by a deep-seated love for the souls that inhabit this terrestrial plain. His role is not one of a distant deity but an intimate mentor, weaving threads of spiritual evolution into the fabric of human existence. He was joined by other creator souls to lower their vibrational levels so they could incarnate and help assist the early humans.

The conflict began because Jehovah decided to step in, tell the struggling humans that he can help them if they worshiped him as their god and creator.

Lucifer and several dozen other technicians figured this wasn't going to allow the earthlings to process and find ways of dealing with the negative energy. This put Lucifer in conflict with Jehovah, and because so many humans were sent into slavery, pledging fealty to what is, in essence, a creator technician, an engineer with a definite psychosis. Simply read the bible, and it's obvious Jehovah is very mentally ill.

This is explained in the book series by Shapiro, and I urge you to read it.

In this area, I happen to be a co-creator spirit, a so-called Blueprint designer. My guide, Daniel, is one as well. Daniel refers to me, and the dozens of others, who descended to earth to incarnate and bring humanity back into line with the experiment. I was told all about this in 2002, before finding the book and reading that account.

This is how I know a good deal about this aspect of Lucifer. It's why I can easily run a meditation, ask him for help, and he'll help me. And his help is almost instantaneous.

THE UNIQUE PERSPECTIVE AND ABILITIES OF LUCIFER THE CREATOR GOD

Now, let's venture further into the distinctive viewpoint and capabilities that define Lucifer in his cosmic role as a Creator God. To grasp this, picture yourself as an observer of the cosmos, gazing upon the intricate dance of galaxies and stars.

Lucifer's perspective transcends the confines of earthly limitations. He perceives the cosmos as both a masterpiece and an ongoing creation, akin to an ever-evolving canvas where the strokes of creation are never truly finished. From his cosmic vantage point, the constructs of time and space dissolve, and the boundaries of reality become fluid.

Imagine Lucifer as the cosmic visionary, with the ability to perceive the intricate interplay of energies and consciousness throughout the cosmos. His awareness extends to the farthest reaches of existence, and his comprehension of the grand design remains unmatched.

Consider his abilities as those of a cosmic alchemist, capable of transmuting cosmic energies and intricately weaving them into the tapestry of creation. He exists beyond the confines of conventional physics, wielding the power to shape and mold the very essence of reality.

In this cosmic role, Lucifer's influence stretches far beyond the limits of Earth. He serves as a cosmic beacon, guiding the evolution of sentient beings across the cosmos. His wisdom and guidance are sought after by entities from distant worlds, drawn to his cosmic perspective and unrivaled capabilities.

Now that I've unveiled the concept of Lucifer as a Creator God, a being whose role extends far beyond the boundaries of our universe, let’s look at the powerful magik on can work with this aspect.

His cosmic perspective and extraordinary abilities

challenge conventional understanding, urging us to broaden our horizons and embark on an exploration of the profound mysteries that enshroud his enigmatic persona.

In a summary of his powers, I'll keep this brief because it's easiest to say "Lucifer the Creator God has the same magik manifestation powers of ***ANY*** god."

Utilizing my own relationship with this aspect and considering its relaxed nature, I have incorporated it into my work. Nonetheless, my main priority is to guarantee that as you explore this aspect, you can effectively attain the desired outcome, while avoiding any potential disruptions that may arise from encountering an unfavorable manifestation of Lucifer's energy.

Now, let's venture further into the distinctive viewpoint and capabilities that define Lucifer in his cosmic role as a Creator God. To grasp this, picture yourself as an observer of the cosmos, gazing upon the intricate dance of galaxies and stars.

Lucifer's perspective transcends the confines of earthly limitations. He perceives the cosmos as both a masterpiece and an ongoing creation, akin to an ever-evolving canvas where the strokes of creation are never truly finished. From his exouniverse vantage point, the constructs of time and space dissolve, and the boundaries of reality become fluid.

Imagine Lucifer as the cosmic visionary, with the

ability to perceive the intricate interplay of energy and consciousness throughout the cosmos. His awareness extends to the farthest reaches of existence, and his comprehension of the grand design remains unmatched.

Now, let's consider his abilities as those of a cosmic alchemist, capable of transmuting cosmic energies and intricately weaving them into the tapestry of creation. Unbound by the limitations of conventional physics, he possesses the extraordinary power to shape and mold the very essence of reality itself. Time is no obstacle for him, as both the past and the future are instantly accessible at his command.

In this exouniverse role, Lucifer's influence stretches far beyond the limits of Earth. He serves as a cosmic beacon, guiding the evolution of sentient beings across the cosmos. His wisdom and guidance are sought after by entities from distant realities, drawn to his cosmic perspective and unrivaled capabilities.

Remember, this is a being whose role extends far beyond the boundaries of our universe. His cosmic perspective and extraordinary abilities challenge conventional understanding, urging us to broaden our horizons and embark on an exploration of the profound mysteries that enshroud his enigmatic persona.

Before I let you go into the ritual itself, we have to be

prepared. It's rare that we get the chance to commune and work with such a powerful being. Unlike powerful daemonic beings, where the slightest mis-step or incomplete thought dooms the magik, or causes the magik to rebound, causing harm or injury, this aspect of Lucifer is quite benevolent.

PREPARATIONS

To prepare for the following rituals, it's my advice to fully understand what it is you want, and how it might arrive. Then, you need to understand that this aspect of Lucifer is more than just a spirit to contact to ask for favors.

After these preparations, you'll be able to run a ritual to commune with Lucifer. You'll learn to recognize this particular energy, to gain awareness of when he draws near, and learn to hear Lucifer counsel you on the path towards your desire.

This aspect is far more useful to help one gain enlightenment than any other power.

This is the true definition of High Magik, to attain a degree of enlightenment, to reach further, raise the level of your own awareness, then to be able to merge your energy with that of a Creator God, accomplishing a great deal in a short amount of time.

Unlike some other magik texts, I will not tell you what you have to wear, or eat, or wash with specific oils. This is straightforward, powerful magik.

What, you might ask, does this aspect get from us?

Lucifer, creator god, wants humans to become enlightened. He wants us to become higher versions of our best selves. This aspect wants us to become self-sufficient, turn away from worshiping any deity, and from this spirit's perspective, a bit of magikal assistance is nothing compared to the amount of energy needed to create entire universes. For this aspect of Lucifer, the act of helping those who call upon him is done from a God-loving point of view. It is given freely and with no conditions.

This aspect will not cause you any harm what-so-ever. This aspect reaches forth to help us with nothing but powerful love in his heart for all humans and all creation.

For a full ritual, which is not really needed, you will need a few white candles, incense that you find pleasing, and a semi-darkened room.

Your petition may be written on any paper, using any pen. A copy of the Creator God sigil and peace and quiet to work the ritual.

RITUAL TO LUCIFER THE CREATOR GOD

To make sure you get this aspect, you can't simply utter his ENN and expect the creator god to arrive. Unlike the egregore or daemonic aspects, this powerful aspect will arrive only after a unique summoning.

Relax, it's quite easy.

The summoning is in an ancient language, tuned to fit our human voice boxes, and is a simple phrase: "Ach nomin, Par Lacha, viz nomnie." Pronounced **ACK NOM-IN PAR LAK-HA VEE NOM-IN-KNEE.** Pronounced exactly as I have written it.

By using this specific phrase, we activate our higher self, causing our vibrational level and awareness to temporarily elevate. As a result, we are able to engage with a particular aspect of Lucifer, and this process establishes an energetic portal through which this aspect can actively participate in our physical reality.

This is really all this ritual needs. Everything thing else is for our own subconscious, to help us know we're working magik and to step out of the way and allow the results to manifest.

Items needed:

A white altar candle to represent the Creator God's pure aspects.*

Ritual specific candle (see appendix for color associations)

Incense to facilitate a sacred atmosphere.*

Lucifer Creator God Sigil (Appendix)*

Crystals like clear quartz or selenite to amplify the energies.

Your petition*

Offering and offering bowl or glass*

This is as simple as I can make it and remains quite effective. Think of it as a template, and just customize it to fit your needs.

As we are working with a powerful spirit, you do not need to concern yourself with astronomical alignments, and work the ritual when the time is best for you. Many of the items suggested are just that: suggestions. Non-optional items are marked at an (*)

When ready, light the incense charcoal or stick. Then light the altar candles and save lighting the ritual candle until it's time to light it after it is blessed by Lucifer.

Cast a simple circle (appendix). Once this has been done, proceed with the summoning:

Say:

Ach nomin, Par Lacha, viz nomnie.

Ach nomin, Par Lacha, viz nomnie.

Lucifer, Creator God, I ask that you join with

me!

Lucifer, Creator God, raise my vibration
So that I may commune with thee!
Ach nomin, Par Lacha, viz nomnie.
Lucifer, Creator God, be with me!

Pause a few moments and await the subtle shifts in the room's air that may indicate that Lucifer, Creator God, has arrived. The presence both comforting, and somewhat warming. I personally taste the energy; it has a copper taste or feel.

Pick up your petition and read over it. Then, read it out loud.

Once you have read your petition, pause a few moments. Visualize the intended outcome. Try to see as much detail as you can. Try to bring up the emotions associated with your desire being fulfilled.

Once you have done this, pick up the sigil you made from the petition, if you have one (if not, skip ahead to the candle). Hold this sigil in one hand, and trace over the lines with your other hand, then ask:

"Oh, great Creator God, Lucifer, I implore you to bless and empower this sigil, enabling the manifestation of my heartfelt desire in my life."

Once this is done, pick up the candle for this desire, and hold it up. Then say:

"Great Lucifer, Creator of all! I now ask that you bless this candle to bring to me my desire, so that it may manifest in my life!"

At this point, it's time for the offering. I suggest a libation of red wine. If doing good works in Lucifer's name, simply tell him what you intend to do. Otherwise, pour a small amount of the wine into the offering bowl, and set it on his sigil.

Say: **"I now humbly offer to you, Great Lucifer, this wine (or whatever it is) in gratitude for acting on my petition!"**

If doing good works, say "Lucifer, I will be ________________________ in your honor, please accept this as my offering, in you name."

The ritual is finished at this point.

You can close the ritual in any way you feel you need to close it, or use my method. What I do is, I hold my hands out over the ritual sigil, candle and Lucifer's sigil. I then imagine energy, gold or silver, flowing through my body and into my hands, then unto the sigil, candle, or other ritual items. I'll then say something like:

"Into this sigil, into this magik candle, I direct

great powers. Power drawn from Lucifer himself, and power drawn from my own higher self, to energize and enchant these symbols to achieve the manifestation of my desire!"

Hold this a few breaths. Really hit these items with this energy.

To finish the ritual, say something like **"This circle now open, but never broken!"**

Snuff out the altar candles and allow the ritual candle to burn completely. Do this safely!

Wait overnight to dispose of the offering. Wine can be poured out onto the ground. Sweets can be left in nature. If doing good works, plan to try to do this within a fortnight (14 days or two weeks, etc) from the end of the ritual.

PATHWORKING LUCIFER THE CREATOR GOD

As explained earlier, to work this type of ritual, you will need a space where you can work undisturbed, plus it's best to have Lucifer's Creator sigil nearby, as well as your desire, written out and ready to read.

This is easily done in a darkened room. Light a single candle in the darkness. Incense is optional.

Step 1: Preparation

Find a quiet and comfortable space where you won't

be disturbed. Dim the lights and sit in a relaxed position. Take several deep breaths to center yourself and clear your mind.

Step 2: Visualization

Close your eyes and imagine yourself suspended in the vast expanse of space, surrounded by swirling galaxies and stars. Feel the cosmic energy all around you as you drift further and further into the cosmos.

Step 3: The Edge of the Universe

As you continue your journey through the cosmos, you reach the edge of the universe. Here, you see swirling star dust and cosmic energies converging. From this cosmic maelstrom, a radiant figure begins to materialize, and it is Lucifer, the Creator God.

Step 4: Approaching Lucifer

Slowly approach Lucifer, who emanates a warm and welcoming energy. His presence is both awe-inspiring and comforting. As you draw nearer, you feel a profound sense of connection and understanding.

Step 5: Asking Your Questions or Making Your Request

Stand before Lucifer and speak your questions or

make your request with sincerity and clarity. Whether you seek guidance, wisdom, or a specific favor, express your intentions openly and honestly. Lucifer listens attentively, his cosmic eyes filled with ancient wisdom.

Step 6: Receiving Guidance

As you communicate with Lucifer, be receptive to the insights and wisdom that flow from his being. His responses may come as thoughts, feelings, or vivid images in your mind. Trust your intuition and the connection you've established.

Step 7: Reading Your Petition

If you have prepared a petition, you may read it aloud to Lucifer. Know that he is already aware of your desires, but verbally expressing them deepens the connection and reinforces your intent.

Step 8: Gratitude

Before you depart, express your gratitude to Lucifer for his presence and guidance. Feel a sense of reverence and appreciation for the cosmic wisdom you've encountered.

Step 9: Return

Slowly begin your journey back from the edge of the universe, retracing your steps through the cosmos. As you return to your physical space, bring with you the insights, guidance, or favor you've received from Lucifer.

Step 10: Grounding

Open your eyes and take a few moments to ground yourself. Write down any insights or messages you received during the pathworking for future reflection.

As soon as you can, pour a small libation for Lucifer, Creator God, and place it on his sigil for 24 hours.

Closing Thoughts:

This pathworking to Lucifer the Creator God is a unique and personal journey. It connects you with the cosmic forces of creation and allows you to tap into your own abilities as a co-creator. Remember that you can revisit this pathworking whenever you seek inspiration, guidance, or a deeper connection with the Creator aspect of Lucifer.

LUCIFER THE CREATOR GOD AND THE LAW OF ATTRACTION

In magik and metaphysics, the concept of vibration plays a pivotal role in manifesting desires and shaping one's reality. It is believed that everything in the universe vibrates at a specific frequency, including our thoughts, emotions, and intentions. To harness the power of the Law of Attraction, one must align their own vibrational frequency with their desires. This is where the enigmatic aspect of Lucifer, the Creator God, comes into play as a profound catalyst for transformation.

Understanding the Law of Attraction:

The Law of Attraction is a universal principle that asserts, "like attracts like." It posits that the energies and frequencies we emit through our thoughts, emotions, and beliefs are mirrored back to us by the universe. In essence, we attract experiences, people, and circumstances that resonate with our dominant vibrational state. To manifest our desires, we must learn to raise our vibration and maintain a frequency that matches the reality we wish to create.

Lucifer the Creator God: A Cosmic Visionary:

Lucifer, in his aspect as the Creator God, offers a unique perspective on the nature of reality and the power of manifestation. Visualize Lucifer as a cosmic visionary, gazing upon the tapestry of existence with profound insight. From his vantage point at the edge of the universe, he perceives the intricate dance of energies and consciousness that weave the fabric of reality.

Lucifer's awareness extends beyond the boundaries of time and space, transcending the limitations of earthly perceptions. In his cosmic wisdom, he recognizes that the universe is not static but in a perpetual state of creation. He understands that the key to manifestation lies in aligning one's own vibration with the desired outcome.

Elevating Vibration through Alignment:

To elevate one's vibration to match a desire, one must first clarify and define that desire with utmost precision. Lucifer encourages us to delve deep into the root of our desires, uncovering the true essence of what we seek. This process involves introspection, meditation, and self-awareness. By understanding our desires on a profound level, we can align our thoughts and emotions with them more effectively.

Once the desire is defined, the next step is to cultivate the vibrational state that resonates with it. Lucifer, as a cosmic alchemist, teaches us the art of transmutation. We can transmute lower vibrational energies, such as doubt, fear, or negativity, into higher, more harmonious frequencies. This transformation involves a shift in mindset, belief systems, and emotional states.

The Role of Visualization and Affirmation:

Lucifer encourages us to use the power of visualization and affirmation in this process. Through focused meditation and creative visualization, we can vividly imagine ourselves already in possession of our desires. This act of mental creation sends out a powerful vibration that aligns with the desired outcome.

Affirmations, carefully crafted statements that affirm our intentions, further reinforce the vibrational alignment. By repeating positive affirmations regularly, we program our subconscious mind to accept our desires as a reality. Lucifer emphasizes the importance of affirmations as a tool to strengthen our vibrational resonance with our desires.

In the pursuit of manifesting our desires through the Law of Attraction, Lucifer, the Creator God, serves as a cosmic mentor and guide. His wisdom teaches us to align our vibration with our intentions by delving into the essence of our desires, transmuting lower energies, and using visualization and affirmation as powerful tools.

By working with Lucifer in this aspect, we embark on a journey of self-discovery and self-mastery. We learn to navigate the intricacies of the vibrational universe and consciously shape our reality. As we elevate our vibration to match our desires, we unlock the transformative potential of the Law of Attraction and witness the manifestation of our dreams in the tapestry of existence.

Pathworking to Align Vibration with Lucifer, the Creator

God

I channeled this simple pathworking from my good friend Lucifer, and it's designed to help you align your vibration with your desires or goals by connecting with the wisdom and energy of Lucifer, the Creator God. Find a quiet and comfortable space where you won't be disturbed, and let's begin.

Step 1: Preparation

Sit or lie down in a relaxed position. Take a few deep breaths to center yourself. Close your eyes and visualize a radiant starry sky, as if you are at the edge of the universe, surrounded by cosmic wonders.

Step 2: Invocation

Using Lucifer, Creator God's unique summoning, say or whisper: "Ach nomin, Par Lacha, viz nomnie, Lucifer, I invite your presence and guidance," invoking Lucifer's energy and presence. Imagine a gentle, warm light descending from the stars above, enveloping you in a comforting glow.

Step 3: Clarify Your Desire

With Lucifer's energy surrounding you, take a moment to clearly define your desire or goal. It could be related to any aspect of your life, such as career, relationships, health, or personal growth. Imagine this desire as a radiant light within you, glowing with potential.

Step 4: Align Your Vibration

Visualize this radiant light of desire merging with the light of Lucifer's presence. As the two energies combine, feel a harmonious resonance building within you. This resonance represents your alignment with your desire.

Step 5: Affirmation

In this aligned state, repeat a simple affirmation that affirms your intention. For example, if your desire is to find a fulfilling career, you might say, "I am now aligned with a fulfilling and prosperous career path." Feel the truth of this statement as you say it.

Step 6: Gratitude

Express gratitude to Lucifer, the Creator God, for his guidance and assistance in aligning your vibration with your desire. Feel a sense of appreciation for the cosmic wisdom and energy that surrounds you.

Step 7: Return

Slowly bring your awareness back to your physical surroundings. Open your eyes when you are ready. Know that you carry the aligned vibration of your desire with you as you continue your journey.

This simple pathworking serves to connect with Lucifer, the Creator God, and harness the power of vibrational alignment. By clarifying your desires and merging your energy with Lucifer's cosmic wisdom, you create a resonance that can positively influence the manifestation of your goals and aspirations. Practice this pathworking regularly to maintain your vibrational alignment and stay attuned to your desires.

CHAPTER 4

THE CONCEPT OF EGREGORES

Imagine, for a moment, the power of collective thought. Picture it as a canvas upon which our beliefs, emotions, and desires are painted in vivid strokes. This shared mental landscape is where egregores, those mystical entities, are born. They are thought-forms given life by the harmonious chorus of countless minds, a concept that transcends the boundaries of individuality and taps into the very essence of our interconnected consciousness.

As we look into the mystical world of egregores, let us first understand their genesis. Consider egregores as thought-beings, entities shaped by the shared intentions and emotional resonance of a group of believers. These entities are not bound by physical form but exist as potent conglomerates of psychic energy, a testament to the profound effect that human collective consciousness can have on the metaphysical tapestry of our existence.

Egregores begin their existence as mere whispers of intention, ethereal threads woven together by those who share common beliefs, goals, or ideals. It is this collective intent that breathes life into them, much like an artist's brush bringing a canvas to life with each stroke. These thought-forms, as they emerge from the collective mind, possess an inherent sense of purpose, often aligned with the shared aspirations of their creators. They are the embodiment of our desires, dreams, and ideologies given form in the ethereal sphere, waiting to exert their influence on our world.

To comprehend egregores fully, we must grasp the role of the collective consciousness in their formation. Think of it as a grand collaboration, where the thoughts, emotions, and intentions of individuals converge to shape a collective vision. In essence, we are the etheric architects of these entities, contributing our beliefs and energy to construct the scaffolding upon which egregores stand.

The process begins with a shared belief system, a unifying ideology that binds individuals together. Whether it's a religious faith, a political ideology, or a cultural tradition, this common ground becomes the foundation upon which the egregore is built. Each believer contributes their thoughts and emotions to this mental edifice, reinforcing the entity's presence.

Imagine a grand cathedral constructed over centuries by countless artisans, each adding their unique touch to the intricate design. Similarly, egregores are the culmination of the collective efforts of their creators, shaped and refined through generations of shared belief. As more minds align with the egregore's purpose, its influence grows, and it gains a degree of autonomy within the psychic world.

Now, let's explore a fundamental aspect of egregores that sets them apart from mere concepts or ideas: their capacity for independent existence. Consider them as living thoughts, entities that not only embody our collective beliefs, but can also act upon them. This is where the mystical nature of egregores truly shines.

Imagine a wildfire sparked by a single ember, gradually spreading and consuming everything in its path. Similarly, egregores possess the ability to propagate and grow through the collective consciousness. Once conceived, they take on a life of their own, influencing the thoughts and actions of their believers.

These living thoughts have a certain level of autonomy within the psychic world. They can guide and inspire their followers, offering insights, protection, or assistance aligned with their purpose. This autonomy allows them to adapt to changing circumstances and continue to serve their believers' needs.

To truly grasp the concept of egregores, one must recognize the pivotal role of belief in their sustenance and strength. It is the unwavering faith of their devotees that breathes life into these thought-forms and empowers them to manifest change in the physical world.

Think of belief as the nourishment that sustains an egregore, much like sunlight and water sustain a flourishing garden. The more fervently individuals believe in the entity's existence and purpose, the more potent it becomes. It's a symbiotic relationship, where belief feeds the egregore's power, and in return, the egregore offers guidance, protection, or blessings to its followers.

Consider the ancient gods and goddesses of mythology, revered by cultures for millennia. These deities are egregores shaped by the collective faith and devotion of countless generations. Their influence on human history, culture, and spirituality is a testament to the profound impact that egregores can have on our world.

Now, let us journey deeper into the mysterious nature of egregores. These thought-forms exist in a dimension that straddles the boundary between the metaphysical and the tangible, a place where belief bridges the gap between the two worlds.

Picture it as a veil, a thin, diaphanous curtain separating our mundane reality from the ethereal domain of egregores. Belief acts as the key to parting this veil, allowing us to commune with these entities and draw upon their power.

Imagine standing before this veil, your beliefs and intentions serving as the incantation that beckons an egregore to your side. As you speak your desires and align your thoughts, the veil shimmers, and the egregore's presence becomes palpable. It is through this mystical interaction that we harness the power of egregores, invoking their aid in our endeavors.

To understand the full scope of egregores, envision a vast, interconnected web of belief. Each egregore is a thread within this intricate tapestry, woven into existence by the collective consciousness of its followers.

Think of this collective web as a living repository of human thought, emotion, and intention. It spans cultures, religions, and ideologies, interconnecting egregores from different corners of the world. The threads of this web carry the imprints of countless generations, preserving the wisdom, hopes, and dreams of humanity.

Imagine tracing a thread within this web, following the beliefs and intentions of those who have contributed to an egregore's existence. As you inquire deeper, you uncover the rich tapestry of human experience, interwoven with the essence of these thought-forms.

In our exploration of egregores, it becomes evident that they are not solitary entities but part of a larger cosmic tapestry, a testament to the intricate interplay between human belief and the metaphysical realms.

Now, let us turn our attention to the rituals and ceremonies that strengthen the connection between believers and egregores. These sacred practices serve as the conduits through which believers channel their intentions and devotion, reinforcing the egregore's presence and influence.

Imagine a group of worshipers gathered in solemn reverence, their rituals a symphony of belief and intention. Through chants, prayers, offerings, and symbolic actions, they amplify their connection to the egregore, deepening their spiritual bond.

Consider these rituals as the threads that weave the egregore into the fabric of human experience. Each act of devotion strengthens the egregore's influence, allowing it to extend its metaphysical reach and provide blessings, guidance, or protection to its followers.

In essence, rituals are the bridge that unites the mundane with the mystical, transforming belief into tangible connection and communion with the egregore.

As we continue our journey into the heart of

egregores, it's essential to understand that each of these thought-forms has a unique purpose or mission. They are not indiscriminate entities, but serve specific roles defined by the collective intentions of their followers.

Imagine an egregore as a guardian spirit, diligently watching over those who invoke its presence. Some egregores may exist to offer protection in times of danger, while others guide seekers on the path to enlightenment. Their purpose is intricately tied to the beliefs and desires of their devotees.

Consider the myriad roles that egregores can assume within the collective consciousness. Some may inspire artistic creativity, while others lend strength in times of adversity. It is the alignment of purpose between believers and egregores that solidifies their bond and allows these entities to fulfill their designated roles.

Egregores are not static entities but dynamic beings that evolve in response to the changing beliefs and needs of their followers. This adaptability is a testament to their resilience and enduring influence.

Imagine an egregore as a chameleon, capable of shifting its form and attributes to meet the evolving aspirations of its devotees. As the collective consciousness of a group transforms, so too does the egregore, aligning itself with the shifting tides of belief.

Consider the way in which ancient gods and goddesses

have adapted over time, taking on new roles and characteristics to remain relevant in the hearts and minds of believers. This ability to evolve ensures that egregores continue to serve as sources of inspiration, guidance, and empowerment throughout the ages.

In our exploration of egregores, we uncover a profound mystical connection that transcends the boundaries of the physical world. It is a connection forged through belief, intention, and shared purpose, binding believers to these thought-forms in ways that defy conventional understanding.

Imagine this connection as a luminous thread of energy, weaving its way through the tapestry of human consciousness. It is a bridge that allows believers to tap into the wisdom, power, and blessings of the egregore, drawing upon its metaphysical presence.

Consider the moments when individuals invoke an egregore's aid, feeling the resonance of their intentions and the ethereal response of the entity. It is a reminder that the mystical connection between believers and egregores is a tangible reality, a testament to the limitless potential of human belief.

LUCIFER THE EGREGORE

Now, here's a question: Is Lucifer an egregore?

Yes, there is an aspect of Lucifer that I consider to be an egregore. This aspect bridges the gap between the

Lightbringer and Creator God aspects and the darker, Daemonic aspects.

Alright, folks, let's dive into this fascinating topic - considering an aspect of Lucifer as an egregore or a collective thought-form. Now, picture this: Lucifer is not just a figure from literature or religious texts, but a dynamic entity that's been shaped and reshaped by countless people's beliefs, stories, and energies over centuries.

So, what we're looking at here is like a massive, evolving art project where generations have added their own brush strokes, creating a multifaceted entity that embodies a range of attributes. These could be anything from the qualities of a light-bringer to a rebel figure, or even a symbol of intellectual enlightenment.

Now, when groups or individuals focus their energies and thoughts on Lucifer, be it through rituals, meditations, or other forms of engagement, they kind of fuel this entity, giving it more power and nuance. It's like adding more layers to the painting, making it even richer and more complex.

When we talk about engaging with this egregore in your magikal practices, it's like having a conversation with a figure that holds the wisdom, energies, and narratives collected over centuries. It's a bit like tapping into a vast database of knowledge and energy, and using it to foster personal growth, knowledge, or empowerment.

So, imagine interacting with this entity as a vibrant, dynamic exchange where you can explore, learn, and perhaps even transform your own perspectives and energies. It's a rich and exciting territory in the field of high magik, offering a lot of room for exploration and development.

So, in a nutshell, thinking of Lucifer as an egregore is all about viewing this figure as a living, breathing collective artwork that's brimming with potential and insights, all set for you to explore in your magikal journey. It's a truly dynamic and interactive process, and I hope you find it as exciting as I do!

Over the centuries, the figure of Lucifer has indeed undergone many transformations in different cultural and religious contexts. Initially stemming from religious scriptures, the figure has been reinterpreted, adapted, and even romanticized in various forms of literature, art, and philosophical discourses. These reinterpretations have not only broadened the perception of Lucifer but have also contributed to the weaving of a rich and intricate tapestry of narratives surrounding him. Each thread of this tapestry represents a unique aspect or interpretation, contributing to a multifaceted and dynamic entity that has been molded and remolded through different epochs and lenses.

This accumulation of various attributes, tales, and perspectives around him has effectively given rise to a potent egregore, an entity that is more than the sum of its parts. This collective thought-form vibrates with energies of rebellion, representing the archetype of the ultimate nonconformist. Additionally, it embodies light-bringing qualities, acting as a beacon of enlightenment and individual empowerment. In some narratives, Lucifer stands as a figure of intellectual pursuit, encouraging individuals to seek knowledge and wisdom, breaking free from the shackles of ignorance. This ever-evolving egregore thrives on the diverse energies and narratives it absorbs, continuously reshaping and redefining itself through the lens of those who engage with it.

Depending on the narratives and energies it has absorbed over time, this egregore offers a rich and expansive platform for exploration in the field of high magik. As an entity that encourages individualism, it beckons practitioners to forge their own paths, to question the established norms, and to seek their own truth. Engaging with this egregore can be seen as a journey of personal transformation, where individuals are encouraged to step into their power, embracing the multifaceted and complex nature of existence.

Moreover, the Luciferian egregore serves as a catalyst for fostering a deeper understanding of the self and the universe, offering a space where wisdom meets curiosity, and where enlightenment is pursued through personal experiences and explorations. Thus, delving into the complexities of this egregore provides a rich and profound path for those venturing into the amazing world of high magik, offering not only a source of knowledge and empowerment but also a space for personal growth and transformation.

Over the centuries, the figure of Lucifer has indeed undergone numerous transformations in different cultural and religious contexts. Initially stemming from religious scriptures, the figure has been reinterpreted, adapted, and even romanticized in various forms of literature, art, and philosophical discourses. These reinterpretations have not only broadened the perception of Lucifer but have also contributed to the weaving of a rich and intricate tapestry of narratives surrounding him. Each thread of this tapestry represents a unique aspect or interpretation, contributing to a multifaceted and dynamic entity that has been molded and remolded through different epochs and lenses.

This accumulation of various attributes, tales, and perspectives around him has effectively given rise to a potent egregore, an entity that is more than the sum of its parts. The energies of rebellion are vibrated by this collective thought-form, thereby representing the archetype of the ultimate nonconformist. Additionally, it embodies light-bringing qualities, acting as a beacon of enlightenment and individual empowerment. In some narratives, Lucifer stands as a figure of intellectual pursuit, encouraging individuals to seek knowledge and wisdom, breaking free from the shackles of ignorance. This ever-evolving egregore thrives on the diverse energies and narratives it absorbs, continuously reshaping and redefining itself through the lens of those who engage with it.

POWERS OF LUCIFER THE EGREGORE

Much like the other aspects, this aspect houses all the other "powers", but here this magik of a specific sort, the magik that is specific to Lucifer, is that of being a catalyst. We need to understand how this plays out using Lucifer. Just as a catalyst initiates and accelerates chemical reactions, Lucifer serves as a metaphysical catalyst, igniting the flames of transformation and illumination within the practitioner's spiritual landscape.

Imagine Lucifer as the spark that ignites the furnace of your inner power. His presence awakens dormant potentials and kindles the fire of magik within. It's this catalytic power that draws magicians and occultists to seek his aid in their rituals, for he is the harbinger of change and enlightenment.

One of Lucifer's most renowned magik powers is his ability to illuminate the hidden paths of knowledge and self-discovery. Think of him as a celestial torchbearer, guiding practitioners through the labyrinthine corridors of the occult and the mysteries of the self.

Imagine yourself standing in a pitch-black maze, unsure of which way to turn. Then, the radiant presence of Lucifer appears, casting a warm, inviting light that reveals the intricate twists and turns of the maze. With each step guided by his magik, you uncover profound insights and hidden truths that were once obscured by darkness.

Lucifer's role as the illuminator is not confined to the external world of magik; it extends to the inner realms of the psyche. He helps practitioners explore the depths of their subconscious, bringing to light the hidden aspects of their being and facilitating transformative self-discovery.

The Master of Alchemy

Lucifer's mastery of magical powers extends into the depths of alchemy, a mystical art centered on transmutation and transformation. In this metaphorical journey, envision Lucifer as the grand alchemist, capable of turning the leaden aspects of life into precious spiritual gold.

Imagine the process of inner alchemy, where the base metals of ignorance and limitation undergo the intense fires of spiritual refinement. In this process, Lucifer's presence is likened to the alchemical furnace, where the impurities of the soul are incinerated, leaving behind a purified and enlightened self.

In this analogy, the practitioner becomes the alchemical vessel, and Lucifer assumes the role of the guiding hand that orchestrates the transformative process. Through his magik, the mundane is transmuted into the sacred, and the seeker ascends to a higher state of existence.

Lucifer's magik powers extend into the forbidden spheres of occult knowledge and esoteric wisdom. Imagine him as the guardian of the hidden scrolls, the keeper of arcane secrets that have been concealed from the profane world.

Think of these secrets as locked doors within the labyrinth of magik, doors that only Lucifer can unlock. He grants access to the forbidden knowledge, allowing the practitioner to peer behind the veils of reality and glimpse the mysteries that lie beyond.

Consider the seeker's journey as a quest for these elusive truths, with Lucifer as the enigmatic guide who leads them through the threshold of the unknown. It is through his magik that the practitioner gains insights and revelations that defy conventional understanding.

Lucifer's magik powers are not limited to external manifestations, but encompass the profound realm of personal transformation. Imagine him as the master of metamorphosis, guiding the practitioner through a process of profound inner change.

Think of this transformation as a caterpillar's journey

to becoming a butterfly. Lucifer's magik serves as the chrysalis, enveloping the seeker in a cocoon of spiritual growth and renewal. Through his influence, the practitioner undergoes a profound metamorphosis, shedding old limitations and emerging as a liberated and empowered being.

Think of this process as a rebirth, with Lucifer as the midwife of spiritual evolution. His magik empowers the practitioner to embrace their true potential and awaken to a higher state of consciousness.

One of Lucifer’s extraordinary capabilities within the world of high magik is his talent for harmonizing energies, allowing practitioners to align themselves with the forces that facilitate creation and manifestation. Consider him to be like the conductor of the celestial orchestra, expertly coordinating the interplay of magical energies to manifest the intended results.

Imagine a chaotic orchestra, each instrument playing a different tune. Lucifer's magik serves as the conductor's baton, bringing harmony to the cacophony. Through his influence, the practitioner gains the ability to align their intentions with the universal flow of energy, creating a harmonious resonance that amplifies the effectiveness of their magik.

Consider this alignment as the practitioner's connection to the cosmic symphony of creation, with Lucifer as the guiding maestro. It is through his magik that the practitioner becomes a co-creator of their reality, conducting the symphony of their desires into manifest form.

Lucifer's magik powers extend to the realm of sacred contracts and agreements, both earthly and metaphysical. Think of him as the cosmic notary, overseeing the signing and sealing of spiritual pacts that bind practitioners to their chosen paths.

Imagine these contracts as solemn oaths and agreements, each carrying profound significance in the practitioner's magikal journey. Lucifer's role is to ensure the integrity of these pacts, upholding the promises made and facilitating the exchange of energy and power.

It is worth considering the practitioner as a signatory to these sacred contracts, wherein Lucifer assumes the responsibility of safeguarding their magikal commitments. The practitioner, through their magik, is able to establish a network of support and empowerment by forging bonds with otherworldly entities, divine forces, and spiritual allies.

Lucifer's magik powers also extend into the sphere of personal revelation and self-awareness. Imagine him as the mirror of introspection, reflecting the hidden aspects of the practitioner's psyche and facilitating profound self-discovery.

Think of this process as a journey into the depths of the self, guided by Lucifer's magik. With his influence, the practitioner gains the ability to peer into the mirror of their soul, confronting their fears, desires, and unresolved issues.

By regarding this introspection as a means to achieve personal liberation, one can view Lucifer as the illuminating force that leads us through the enigmatic corners of our own minds. The practitioner is able to attain a deeper understanding of themselves by harnessing his magik, thus unlocking the door to inner wisdom and self-empowerment.

Lucifer's magik powers encompass the guardianship of the inner flame, the divine spark of enlightenment within each practitioner. Imagine him as the eternal flamekeeper, tending to the sacred fire that symbolizes the seeker's inner illumination.

Think of this inner flame as a beacon of divine wisdom and enlightenment, perpetually burning within the practitioner's soul. Lucifer's role is to protect and nourish this flame, ensuring its eternal radiance.

Consider the seeker as the guardian of this inner flame, with Lucifer as the eternal protector. It is through his magik that the practitioner gains the strength to overcome obstacles and adversities, allowing their inner light to shine brightly.

In high magik, Lucifer empowers practitioners to embrace their own sovereignty and take control of their destiny. Imagine him as the empowering mentor, teaching the practitioner the art of self-mastery and self-determination.

Think of this empowerment as the practitioner's ascent to the throne of their own destiny, with Lucifer as the wise guide. Through his magik, the seeker gains the knowledge and confidence to navigate the twists and turns of their life path, becoming the master of their own fate.

You can view this journey as a quest for personal empowerment that the practitioner embarks on, with Lucifer playing the role of the catalyst for their self-realization. It is through his magik that the seeker discovers their inner strength, transcends limitations, and becomes a true magikal adept.

As I conclude my exploration of the magik powers of Lucifer the Egregore, I have unveiled the multifaceted aspects of his influence within the realm of magik. Each point has shed light on a different facet of his power, from catalyzing transformation to facilitating personal revelation. Yet, my journey into the depths of Lucifer's magik is far from over, for there are more revelations and insights awaiting me in the chapters to come.

PREPARATION FOR RITUAL

Preparations for a ritual to Lucifer the Egregore is somewhat similar to the to the preparations for Lucifer the Daemonic. There are some important changes you need to pay attention to when preparing this ritual.

Lucifer the Egregore is more daemonic in nature than

the Lightbringer aspect, but not as dangerous as the full daemonic aspect, so safeguards need to be done prior to working a ritual. I suggest the Daemonic Circle Casting in the appendix. Careful wording of your petition is needed. Pay attention to how the desire is to manifest, namely make sure to say "safely and with harm to none."

This Egregore aspect can bring you most anything, and especially useful in magik for when you need things in a hurry. The Egregore is very useful for speeding things along. For example, if a relationship is unstable, one partner is perhaps abusive of the other, then a "Break up" ritual will help assist the hurt person in the relationship to leave quicker than they'd normally leave.

After careful wording of the petition, a briefer version can be used to craft a sigil. You can activate this sigil during the ritual.

Incense: Most any incense is appropriate. I use frankincense and white copal, or dragon's blood incense. If you are using a stick incense, use non-perfumed incense. Many companies make frankincense but try to locate a brand that is close to the resin frankincense as possible. A brand called Sultanate of Oman makes the best frankincense sticks on the market. Otherwise look for "Mothers Fragrances" or Royal Incense.

Offerings: Think of this aspect as a persona in between the Lightbringer and Daemonic. It's custom to do a blood offering to a daemonic spirit. To do this, have a small print out of the Egregore sigil, and using a diabetic lancet, draw a single drop of blood from a finger (any finger, any hand) and place this on the sigil. Then carefully burn the sigil in a fireproof bowl, making sure the entire sigil is completely burned. Beyond that, a small offering of wine is also acceptable.

LUCIFER THE EGREGORE RITUAL

To make sure you get this aspect, you can simply utter his ENN and expect this aspect to arrive. You need to be prepared by working a Daemonic Circle, casting out non-aligned energies, and making sure you have all the guardians present.

Relax, it's still quite easy.

The standard ENN is a phrase of what appears on the surface to be nonsense words, but are attuned to allow you to get into contact with Lucifer the Egregore. But here, I present a unique summoning designed to call forth the egregore aspect of Lucifer.

This is really all this ritual needs. Everything thing else is for our own subconscious, to help us know we're working magik and to step out of the way and allow the results to manifest.

Items needed:

A black or red altar candle(s) to represent Lucifer's Egregore aspect*

Ritual specific candle (see appendix for color associations)

Incense (preferably frankincense or myrrh) to facilitate a sacred atmosphere. *

Lucifer Egregore Sigil (Appendix)*

Crystals like clear quartz or selenite to amplify the energies.

Your petition*

Diabetic Lancet and fireproof bowl

Or Libation Offering and offering bowl or glass*

This is as simple as I can make it and have it remain effective. Think of it as a template, and just alter to fit your needs.

As we are working with a powerful spirit, you do not need to concern yourself with astronomical alignments and work the ritual when the time is best for you. Many of the items suggested are just that: suggestions. Non-optional items are marked at an (*)

When ready, light the incense charcoal or stick. Then light the altar candles and save lighting the ritual candle until it's time to light it after it is blessed by Lucifer.

Cast a simple circle (appendix). Once this has been done, proceed with the summoning:

Say:

Renich Tasa Uberaca Biasa Icar *Lucifer*!
Renich Tasa Uberaca Biasa Icar *Lucifer*!
I call upon your powerful presence, Lucifer.
With respect and intent, I summon thee,
To share your wisdom and guidance with me.

Pause a few moments and await the subtle shifts in the room's air that may indicate that Lucifer has arrived. This can be the candle flames flickering oddly, the incense smoke behaving abnormally, a heavy presence in the air itself.

Pick up your petition and read over it. Then, read it out loud.

Once you have read your petition, pause a few moments. Visualize the intended outcome. Try to see as much detail as you can. Try to bring up the emotions associated with your desire being fulfilled.

Once you have done this, pick up the sigil you made from the petition, if you have one (if not, skip ahead to the candle). Hold this sigil in one hand, and trace over the lines with your other hand, then ask:

"Oh great Lucifer, I implore you to bless and empower this sigil, enabling the manifestation of my heartfelt desire in my life."

Once this is done, pick up the candle for this desire, and hold it up. Then say:

"Great Lucifer! I now ask that you bless this candle to bring to me my desire, so that it may manifest in my life!"

At this point, it's time for the offering. I suggest a libation of red wine. Or you can do a simple blood offering.

Say: **"I now humbly offer to you, Great Lucifer, this wine (or whatever it is) in gratitude for acting on my petition!"**

If doing a blood offering, prick a finger (any finger and any hand) and put a single drop on his Egregore sigil, then burn the sigil while saying: **"I now humbly offer to you, Great Lucifer, a drop of my essence in gratitude for acting on my petition!"**

Make sure the sigil is completely burned and is just

ashes. Dispose of the ashes outside after the ritual.

The ritual is finished at this point.

You can close the ritual in any way you feel you need to close it or use my method. What I do is, I hold my hands out over the ritual sigil, candle, and Lucifer's sigil. I then imagine energy, gold, or silver, flowing through my body and into my hands, then unto the sigil, candle, or other ritual items. I'll then say something like:

"Into this sigil, into this magik candle, I direct great powers. Power drawn from Lucifer himself, and power drawn from my own higher self, to energize and enchant these symbols to achieve the manifestation of my desire!"

Hold this a few breaths. Really hit these items with this energy.

To finish the ritual, say something like **"This circle now open, but never broken!"**

Snuff out the altar candles and allow the ritual candle to burn completely. Do this safely!

Wait overnight to dispose of the offering. Wine can be poured out onto the ground. Sweets can be left in nature. If doing good works, plan to try to do this within a fortnight (14 days, two weeks, etc) from the end of the ritual.

PATHWORKING THE EGREGORE ASPECT

Although we can easily access the Egregore with a regular ritual, the pathworking is a bit different, enough so that I will include it here.

I have a special sigil for Lucifer, the Egregore, so print this out and have it with you when working this sequence.

Prepare for this pathworking in a quiet and undisturbed space. Light a candle, combining black and white to symbolize the merging of the Daemonic and Fallen Angelic aspects of Lucifer.

Protect yourself

Take a few moments to calm your mind and center yourself. Take several deep breaths. Now, ground yourself by visualizing threads of gold flowing from your feet, or hips if laying down. Send these threads deep into the earth to ground your energy. Next, visualize a beam of iridescent gold light from above, entering the top of your head. This light flows through your body to surround you in a cocoon of protection.

Step 1: The Intersection of Light and Darkness

Visualize yourself standing at the intersection of two contrasting realms, one bathed in radiant light and the other shrouded in deep darkness. This is the meeting point of Lucifer's Daemonic and Fallen Angelic aspects, where a balance of power and knowledge awaits.

Step 2: The Confluence

As you step forward, you enter a space where light and darkness intertwine, creating a harmonious blend of energies. Here, you can sense the presence of Lucifer the Egregore, a being that combines both traits. Approach this presence with reverence and curiosity.

Step 3: Greeting the Egregore

Lucifer the Egregore manifests before you as a figure of captivating beauty and grace, with wings that transition from radiant white to obsidian black. Acknowledge this powerful and enigmatic being with respect.

Engage in a conversation with Lucifer the Egregore. Share your intentions and questions openly, knowing that this aspect possesses both the wisdom of the Fallen Angel and the transformative power of the Daemonic. Seek guidance or insights into your spiritual journey or any specific concerns you may have.

Step 4: The Unveiling

Lucifer the Egregore imparts his knowledge, revealing hidden truths and insights that bridge the realms of light and darkness. It may provide you with a unique perspective on your path, helping you navigate the complexities of life and spirituality.

Be attentive to the wisdom and energy flowing from this merged aspect. Embrace the transformative potential it offers, allowing it to guide you in your spiritual evolution.

Step 5: Departure

As your conversation concludes and you feel you've received the guidance you sought, express your gratitude to Lucifer the Egregore. Step back from the confluence of light and darkness, returning to your physical space.

Blow out the candle, symbolizing the end of your pathworking. Take some time to reflect on the insights and energy you've received from Lucifer the Egregore, a unique aspect that combines the traits of both the Daemonic and the Fallen Angelic, offering a balanced and transformative experience.

Offering:

I suggest you work a simple gratitude ritual once you have completed the pathworking, and signs of your desire are beginning to manifest.

CHAPTER 5

Lucifer the Daemonic

This aspect of Lucifer is perhaps the most used in ritual magik. His daemonic ENN and daemonic sigil will definitely bring you this aspect. And it's one aspect you had better be ready to work protection and carefully word your petition.

Unlike the egregore version, this aspect of Lucifer brings with it serious daemonic power, and this aspect is a crafty, deceptive spirit. Like the egregore, thousands have worked with this aspect, making this the most well-known aspect. As such, the ideals of all the followers have impressed on this aspect the traits normally associated with the more dangerous and powerful daemons.

Explore this aspect with a mix of caution combined with respect. It's a raw power that can cause huge windfalls. And cause the worst kinds of suffering.

In my mind, this aspect mirrors the worst traits of some major religious godheads. Easily angered, somewhat jealous and prone to give you exactly what you ask for, but not what you actually wanted. In this respect, the crafting of the petition is the most important of tasks. Make damned sure the petition spells out what you desire, and even go into some detail about how you wish it delivered, and always make sure to specify "with harm to none."

It's common knowledge that when asking for certain desires, for example, a sudden windfall, the windfall of money might come because of a relative passing away, or legal settlement from an injury lawsuit. This is not the preferred method of receiving a windfall.

Therefore, it's crucial to be specific and clear about the desired outcome, without leaving any room for misinterpretation. This aspect of Lucifer is not for the faint of heart, and those who choose to work with it must be prepared to face the consequences of their actions.

It's important to note that this aspect of Lucifer is not evil, but rather, it embodies the raw power of creation and destruction. It's up to the practitioner to use this power wisely and responsibly, without causing harm to themselves or others.

So, gang, working with this aspect of Lucifer requires caution, respect, and a deep understanding of the power at play. It's a tool that can bring great rewards, but it can also cause immense suffering if used recklessly. Therefore, before delving into this realm of ritual magic, one must be prepared to work with protection and carefully craft their petition to ensure the desired outcome is achieved without causing harm to anyone.

Let me go further on this.

As I take you further into this labyrinthine aspect of Lucifer, additional layers of complexity and caution are unveiled. It's not simply about mastering ritual techniques or accumulating esoteric knowledge; it's a process that demands rigorous self-examination and continual growth. Indeed, this aspect of Lucifer serves as a mirror that reflects the abyss within oneself, making it a compelling but perilous path to self-mastery.

A working relationship with Lucifer the Daemonic can be likened to mastering an ancient and treacherous martial art. One cannot simply learn a few moves and claim expertise; it's a lifelong journey that demands ongoing practice, refinement, and adaptation. For this, many experienced practitioners recommend maintaining a dedicated journal exclusive to your workings with this aspect. Document your petitions, the nuances of the ritual, the omens you received, and the outcomes that followed. Over time, this becomes a crucial database that can help refine your future approaches and, importantly, help you understand the unique 'language' this entity uses to communicate with you.

There is a commonly held misconception that entities like Lucifer the Daemonic can be controlled or enslaved through ritual. This is a grievous error. Such entities are more accurately viewed as potential allies—or adversaries—depending on how one chooses to engage. The balance of power in the relationship is delicate and must be respected. Therefore, negotiation and diplomatic skills become as vital to the practitioner as any athame or pentacle. Consider each interaction as a step in building a complex relationship; small gifts, tokens, or offerings can go a long way in gaining favor but should never be considered as a surefire way to 'buy' loyalty or services.

Moreover, the Daemonic aspect of Lucifer also serves as an initiatory force. It presents you with challenges, puzzles, and moral quandaries designed to test your mettle and provoke your evolution. These could manifest as life events, dreams, or even as shifts in your emotional landscape. In this light, even the 'negative' experiences can become invaluable lessons—if you're willing to learn. Thus, one cannot approach this aspect with a transactional mindset but should embrace a transformational approach.

It's worth mentioning that some magicians employ protective measures that extend beyond the standard ritual protections like salt circles or pentagrams. Psychic shielding, amulets charged with protective spells, and even the involvement of protective deities or guides, are utilized to create a multi-layered defense. This is akin to cybersecurity; the more layers you have, the harder it becomes for any malevolent force to penetrate. Always remember, this is not about mere material gains or transient successes; you're entering into a cosmic contract that can reverberate through your spiritual timeline.

So, to all the intrepid souls willing to explore this tantalizing yet treacherous dimension, be forewarned yet be encouraged. Your journey with Lucifer the Daemonic is not just about mastering an arcane art, but is a profound spiritual voyage. It promises vistas of incredible beauty and abysses of unfathomable darkness. Step wisely, craft your petitions like a maestro, and may your ethical compass be as steadfast as your will. This is a path that can bring transcendental enlightenment or soul-wrenching despair, entirely contingent upon your choices and intent.

Choose wisely. I can’t stress this enough.

TYPES OF MAGIK

This aspect of Lucifer is good for most magik, as long

as you are very careful. This is high risk, high reward. This ideally requires advanced skills in ritual magik and a thorough grounding in protective measures. Below are some magikal workings specifically geared toward this aspect. Remember, these are not for beginners and should be approached with a level of caution and respect commensurate with the entity in question.

Petition for Clarity and Wisdom

One of the less risky endeavors when working with this aspect is to ask for wisdom or clarity about a specific situation. Create a sigil that embodies your question or problem. During the ritual, use dragon's blood ink to draw the Daemonic sigil of Lucifer and place your question sigil over it. Light a black candle anointed with mugwort oil and recite the Daemonic ENN while focusing intensely on your question. Remember to specify that the wisdom should come without harm to anyone and end with a respectful acknowledgment of the entity.

Wealth and Abundance Spell

This working is riskier due to its material focus. Prepare a green candle and anoint it with patchouli or cinnamon oil. Write your petition on a piece of parchment, specifying the form in which you'd like to receive wealth—be as clear as possible to avoid unintended consequences. Place a charged talisman or object that represents wealth to you underneath the candle. Light the candle while reciting Lucifer's Daemonic ENN and focus on your intention. Always close with an acknowledgment and a phrase specifying that the wealth should come "with harm to none."

Daemonic Soul Alchemy

For the bravest and most experienced of practitioners, this is a transformative ritual aimed at accelerating spiritual growth. Prepare your space with the utmost care, ensuring multiple layers of protection. Cast your circle, call the quarters, and place a Scrying mirror on your altar. Light a purple or gold candle anointed with frankincense oil. Recite invocations that request Lucifer's Daemonic aspect to guide you in shedding old spiritual layers and integrating new energies. The aim is to create a magikal crucible in which your soul is both the alchemist and the subject of alchemy. Beware, this can lead to intense life changes and should not be done lightly.

Astral Communion

If you're versed in astral projection, consider meeting this aspect of Lucifer on the astral plane. Establish strong psychic shields and make sure your physical space is warded.

Once on the astral plane, use the Daemonic ENN as a beacon to guide you to this specific aspect. The meeting can be used for various purposes—knowledge exchange, negotiation, or forging an astral pact. Make sure to maintain a strong will and clear boundaries.

When I meet with this aspect, he'll project a setting right out of a Hammer Horror version of Dracula. Dark night, blue clouds, and Lucifer on a rise, long cloak moving slightly in the wind, and - yes - Christopher Lee's visage. Combed back hair, gaunt, blue face, and red eyes. I'm not sure what he thinks he's accomplishing when he does this, but it's a good effect.

Protective Measures

Regardless of the magik you decide to work, always follow strict protective protocols. This can range from simple salt circles and Lesser Banishing Rituals of the Pentagram (LBRP - A version is in the Appendix) to more advanced techniques like constructing astral fortresses or calling upon protective deities or guides.

Remember that working with the Daemonic aspect of Lucifer is not to be taken lightly; the practitioner should be well-versed in occult lore, experienced in ritual magik, and ethically sound. Always keep the axiom "with harm to none" at the forefront of your magikal workings with this potent and complex entity.

PREPARATION FOR RITUAL

A ritual to Lucifer the Daemonic is like the rituals to Lucifer the Egregore. The same exacting precautions must be used.

Make sure your petition is fool proof. Then work again to make it bullet proof. Remember, this aspect of Lucifer delivers to you exactly what you ask for, but precisely not what you really want.

Candles:

I use a mix of black and white as altar candles. Lucifer the Daemonic also loves some red candles on the altar.

Incense:

Think purification when it comes to incense. Frankincense is the very best incense to use in one of these rituals. Obtain a good quality resin. If you want to use stick incense, go with frankincense, and avoid those cheap perfume based incenses often found in smoke shops or in a grocery store.

Offerings:

Lucifer is a traditionalist. As such, be prepared to offer a blood sacrifice. You will need a small daemonic sigil, a diabetic lancet and a fore proof bowl. Follow the directions in the ritual itself.

Otherwise, at first, I was able to get away with a libation to Lucifer. He's agreeable with a high-quality whiskey or spirit, or a very good glass of wine.

BASIC RITUAL TO DAEMONIC LUCIFER

This is a standard ritual to any daemonic spirit. You can change the ritual specific candles to match your desire or goal and change the incense or offering as needed.

To make sure you get this aspect, you can't simply utter his ENN and expect the creator god to arrive. Unlike the egregore or daemonic aspects, this powerful aspect will arrive only after a unique summoning.

Relax, it's quite easy.

The summoning is in an ancient language, tuned to fit our human voice boxes, and is a simple phrase. It is Lucifer's common ENN: *Renich Tasa Uberaca Biasa Icar Lucifer!*

By using this specific phrase, we activate our higher self, causing our vibrational level and awareness to temporarily elevate. As a result, we are able to engage with a particular aspect of Lucifer, and this process establishes an energetic portal through which this aspect can actively participate in our physical reality.

This is really all this ritual needs. Everything thing else is for our own subconscious, to help us know we're working magik and to step out of the way and allow the results to manifest.

Items needed:

White and black altar candles to represent Lucifer's daemonic aspects.*

Ritual specific candle (see appendix for color associations)

Incense (preferably frankincense or myrrh) to facilitate a sacred atmosphere.*

Lucifer Daemonic Sigil (Appendix)*

Crystals like clear quartz or selenite to amplify the energies.

Your petition*

Offering and offering bowl or glass* or

Diabetic lancet and fireproof bowl for blood offering*

This is as simple as I can make it, and it remains quite effective. Think of it as a template, and just alter to fit your needs.

As we are working with a powerful spirit, you do not need to concern yourself with astronomical alignments and work the ritual when the time is best for you.

When ready, light the incense charcoal or stick. Then

light the altar candles and save lighting the ritual candle until it's time to light it after it is blessed by Lucifer.

Cast a daemonic circle (appendix). Once this has been done, proceed with the summoning:

Say:

Renich Tasa Uberaca Biasa Icar Lucifer!
Renich Tasa Uberaca Biasa Icar Lucifer!
I call upon your powerful presence, Lucifer.
With respect and intent, I summon thee,
To share your wisdom and guidance with me.

Pause a few moments and await the subtle shifts in the room's air that may indicate that Lucifer has arrived. I personally taste the energy, it has a copper taste or feel. You may feel his presence by the room getting cooler, or the candle flames dancing. Incense smoke may also act differently.

Pick up your petition and read over it. Then, read it out loud.

Once you have read your petition, pause a few moments. Visualize the intended outcome. Try to see as much detail as you can. Try to bring up the emotions associated with your desire being fulfilled.

Once you have done this, pick up the sigil you made from the petition, if you have one (if not, skip ahead to the candle). Hold this sigil in one hand, and trace over the lines with your other hand, then ask:

"Oh great Lucifer, I implore you to bless and empower this sigil, enabling the manifestation of my heartfelt desire in my life."

Once this is done, pick up the candle for this desire, and hold it up. Then say:

"Great Lucifer, Prince of Darkness! I now ask that you bless this candle to bring to me my desire, so that it may manifest in my life!"

At this point, it's time for the offering. This part is for giving over a drop of blood. Prick a finger, any hand and any finger, and place a single drop of blood onto his sigil. Touch the sigil to a candle, and as it burns, say: **"I now humbly offer to you, Great Lucifer, a drop of my essence in gratitude for acting on my petition!"**

Make sure the sigil is completely burned and is just ashes. Dispose of the ashes outside after the ritual.

If giving an offering of wine, say: **"I now humbly offer to you, Great Lucifer, a libation of _______ in gratitude for acting on my petition."**

The ritual is finished at this point.

You can close the ritual in any way you feel you need to close it or use my method. What I do is, I hold my hands out over the ritual sigil, candle, and Lucifer's sigil. I then imagine energy, gold, or silver, flowing through my body and into my hands, then unto the sigil, candle, or other ritual items. I'll then say something like:

"Into this sigil, into this magik candle, I direct great powers. Power drawn from Lucifer himself, and power drawn from my own higher self, to energize and enchant these symbols to achieve the manifestation of my desire!"

Hold this a few breaths. Really hit these items with this energy.

To finish the ritual, say something like **"This circle now open, but never broken!"**

Snuff out the altar candles, and allow the ritual candle to burn completely. Do this safely!

Wait overnight to dispose of the libation offering. Wine can be poured out onto the ground. Ashes tossed to the winds outside.

Pathworking to Lucifer the Daemonic, the Prince of Darkness:

Before embarking on this pathworking to connect with

Lucifer the Prince of Darkness, find a quiet and secluded space where you can concentrate without disturbances. Light a black candle, signifying the darkness and the hidden aspects of this daemon, and place it in front of you.

Have with you either Lucifer's traditional sigil, or the Daemonic Sigil I created for this book (sigils chapter).

Protect yourself

Take a few moments to calm your mind and center yourself. Take several deep breaths. Now, ground yourself by visualizing threads of gold flowing from your feet, or hips if laying down. Send these threads deep into the earth to ground your energy. Next, visualize a beam of iridescent gold light from above, entering the top of your head. This light flows through your body to surround you in a cocoon of protection.

Step 1: The Descent into Darkness

Next, visualize yourself standing at the edge of a vast, dark abyss. This abyss represents the realm of Lucifer, the Prince of Darkness, where hidden knowledge and power await. In your mind's eye, take a step into the abyss, feeling the cool and mysterious energy surrounding you.

Step 2: The Path of Shadows

As you descend deeper into the abyss, a dimly lit path

begins to materialize before you. Follow this path as it leads you further into the heart of the darkness. With each step, you draw closer to Lucifer, the Prince of Darkness, who resides in the depths of this realm.

Step 3: Confrontation with the Prince of Darkness

In the distance, you sense a powerful presence. It's Lucifer, the Prince of Darkness, concealed in the shadows. Approach with reverence and caution, as this daemon requires careful handling. Stand before the Prince of Darkness and acknowledge its formidable presence. You may feel a sense of awe and trepidation.

Engage in a respectful and mindful conversation with the Prince of Darkness. State your intentions clearly and humbly. Ask that he assist you in manifesting your desires, or ask for his guidance or insights into your spiritual path or any specific matters you seek to understand. Be attentive to the responses, which may come as thoughts, feelings, or subtle signs.

Step 4: Receiving Knowledge and Power

Listen carefully to the Prince of Darkness's wisdom. It may offer you profound insights, hidden knowledge, or even the keys to unlocking your inner potential. This aspect of Lucifer is known for its willingness to assist those who approach it with respect and sincerity. Be open to receiving the gifts it offers.

Step 5: Departure

When you feel that your interaction is complete, express your gratitude to the Prince of Darkness for its presence and guidance. Slowly begin to ascend the path, leaving the abyss behind. As you step out of the darkness, you find yourself back in your physical space.

Blow out the black candle to signify the end of your pathworking. Take some time to reflect on your experience and the knowledge you've gained. Remember that Lucifer the Prince of Darkness is a powerful and enigmatic daemon who can provide valuable insights and assistance when approached with care and reverence.

Offering:

I suggest you work a simple gratitude ritual once you have completed the pathworking, and signs of your desire are beginning to manifest.

CHAPTER 6

BANEFUL MAGIK

Lucifer the Daemonic is very useful for those times when baneful magik is needed.

Baneful magik, as I explore it in this chapter, is a branch of magik that involves working with energies and intentions to bring about specific, often challenging, outcomes. It's a path of magikal practice that deals with the manipulation of energy for purposes that may include hexing, cursing, or causing harm to others. While this might sound ominous, it's essential for you to understand that baneful magik, like any other form of magik, is a tool. How you use it depends entirely on my intent and ethical considerations. Just as a sharp knife can be used for cutting food or for harm, you can employ baneful magik with responsible and ethical intentions. In essence, baneful magik is about harnessing the forces of the metaphysical realm to create change, whether that change is to protect yourself, correct an injustice, or even provoke personal growth. It's a path that requires a deep understanding of energy dynamics, personal responsibility, and ethical considerations, and it's not to be undertaken lightly.

But first:

MINIMIZING NEGATIVE CONSEQUENCES: SAFEGUARDING YOUR JOURNEY

In our pursuit of magik and the exploration of Lucifer in his daemonic aspect, it is of paramount importance to safeguard our journey from negative consequences. Just as a wise traveler prepares for unforeseen challenges on a treacherous path, we must equip ourselves with the techniques and tools to mitigate potential blow-back when working with the daemonic.

Imagine you're a seasoned explorer traversing through uncharted territories. Each step you take carries the potential for both discovery and danger. Similarly, when questing into the daemonic, we are venturing into realms where the energies are potent and the consequences can be unpredictable.

One crucial tool in our arsenal is the establishment of clear boundaries and intentions. Think of these boundaries as the walls of a fortress protecting your magik. When working with the daemonic, it's essential to define the scope and purpose of your magikal endeavors. This clarity acts as a shield, preventing unwanted energies from infiltrating your work.

Consider the analogy of a gardener cultivating a precious flower. The gardener carefully tends to the soil, protects the plant from pests, and ensures it receives the right amount of sunlight and water. Similarly, in magik, we nurture our intentions and protect them from negative influences, creating an environment where they can flourish.

One of the most valuable sources of knowledge in the realm of magik is personal experience. Just as a seasoned sailor learns to navigate treacherous waters through years of practice, we too can glean insights from our encounters with the daemonic. My own journey has been filled with valuable lessons in mitigating blow-back.

Imagine you're a sailor facing a sudden storm at sea. The turbulent waves threaten to capsize your vessel, but your experience guides you in handling the situation. Similarly, when working with the daemonic, unexpected challenges may arise, but your accumulated wisdom becomes your anchor in the tempest.

I have faced moments when the energies invoked during daemonic magik seemed to spiral out of control. These experiences have taught me the importance of grounding techniques. Think of grounding as the anchor that keeps your magik rooted in the physical realm. It allows you to harness the energies without being swept away by their intensity.

My biggest lesson learned wasn't from baneful magik, in and of itself, but a ritual to compel the love of another can be considered baneful. In this instance, I wasn't summoning Lucifer in any aspect, but I was summoning Satan. I am certain Satan got a good laugh at my expense. You see, sometimes when magik is done out of inexperience and naivete, the worse that can happen will be it'll fail and nothing happens. This is a fail-safe in magik where no one gets hurt. No harm, no foul. But in my case, the magik worked. But worked too well, and, dummy me, I kept working the ritual until I had a real mess on my hands. (I share this story in full in my Lilith book.)

Consider the analogy of a blacksmith forging a powerful weapon. The heat of the forge is intense, but the blacksmith's skill and experience ensure that the metal is shaped precisely as desired. Similarly, our experiences in daemonic magik refine our abilities and teach us how to wield these potent energies effectively.

RESPONSIBLE AND ETHICAL USE: THE HEART OF BANEFUL MAGIK

The practice of this specific magik leads us down the path of the shadowy elements within the daemonic realm, thereby demanding a greater level of responsibility and adherence to ethical principles. In the same way that a skilled chef meticulously chooses ingredients and adheres to a recipe, it is essential for us to approach dark magik with caution and a deep understanding of its immense power.

Imagine you're a chef crafting a gourmet dish. Each ingredient contributes to the overall flavor, and a misstep can result in a dish that is unpalatable or even harmful. Similarly, in baneful magik, your intentions and actions must be precise, with a deep understanding of the consequences they may yield.

Responsible use of baneful magik involves considering the ethical implications of our actions. Just as a judge weighs the evidence in a court of law, we must weigh the potential harm and benefit of our magikal endeavors. It's crucial to understand that the daemonic energies can be potent and far-reaching, and using them recklessly can have unintended consequences.

Consider the analogy of a gardener tending to a thorny plant. While the thorns may serve a protective purpose, the gardener handles them with care to avoid harm. How was I to know that cucumbers and squash have thorns? I didn't! Now I use gloves! Similarly, in baneful magik, we must approach our intentions with a sense of responsibility, ensuring that our actions are guided by ethical considerations. You'll need psychic gloves, in other words!

UNDERSTANDING THE CONSEQUENCES OF BANEFUL MAGIK

Just as every action in the physical world has consequences, so, too, does every magikal act in the metaphysical realm. It's essential to grasp that the energy we put into baneful magik carries with it a ripple effect, much like a pebble thrown into a pond, creates expanding waves.

Imagine you're standing at the edge of a tranquil lake. When you toss a pebble into the water, it creates a series of concentric ripples that extend outward. Each ripple represents a consequence of your action, and the larger the pebble, the more significant the impact. Similarly, in baneful magik, our actions send out energetic ripples that can affect not only our intended target but also ourselves.

Understanding these consequences requires a level of awareness and responsibility. Just as a scientist carefully studies the effects of an experiment, we must approach baneful magik with a scientific mindset. This means observing, recording, and analyzing the outcomes of our actions to refine our techniques and intentions.

In this baneful magik, we must anticipate and be prepared for the reactions that may arise from our actions. Although true blow-back is rare, in my experience, unexpected results can, and do happen. You might start out working magik just to "teach a lesson" and if your anger at the subject is great, then more magik will be sent out than you expected. You should approach this type of magik with a clear head, temper your anger, control your energy.

PROTECTION AND WARDING: SAFEGUARDING YOUR MAGIKAL SPACE

While working with this type of magik, it is of utmost importance to possess protection and warding as indispensable tools in our arsenal. Similar to how a knight prepares for battle by putting on armor, we, too, need to strengthen ourselves against possible spiritual or energetic dangers.

Imagine you're a guardian of an ancient castle, responsible for protecting its treasures from invaders. Your role requires vigilance and the use of strategic defenses to deter any intruders. Similarly, in baneful magik, we become guardians of our own spiritual space, and protection becomes our shield.

Protection techniques include creating energetic

barriers, invoking protective entities, and consecrating sacred objects. These practices act as metaphysical shields that help repel negativity and unwanted influences. In essence, they serve as your spiritual armor in the pursuit of baneful magik.

Consider the analogy of a locksmith crafting intricate locks to secure valuable possessions. Each lock is designed to safeguard against unauthorized access. Similarly, we craft our own metaphysical locks and keys to protect our sacred space and intentions.

HARMONIZING WITH THE LAWS OF THE UNIVERSE

Within the boundless expanse of the universe, there exists a complex fabric in which fundamental laws govern the perpetual flow of energy and the very essence of existence. Just like the stars, these laws are unchanging and permanent, and it is crucial for any baneful magik practitioner to comprehend them fully.

Imagine you're a sailor navigating the open sea, relying on the laws of navigation to chart your course. Just as the constellations guide your way, the universal laws guide our magikal journey. Ignoring these laws would be akin to sailing blindly into treacherous waters.

One such law is the Law of Correspondence, which states, "As above, so below; as below, so above." This law reminds us that the macrocosm and microcosm are interconnected, and changes in one realm can affect the other. In baneful magik, this law underscores the importance of understanding the broader implications of our actions.

The Alchemy of Baneful Magik: Transmutation of Energy

Baneful magik involves a unique form of alchemy, where we transmute and manipulate energy to achieve our intentions. This process is akin to the transformation of base metals into precious gold, and it requires a deep understanding of energetic dynamics.

Imagine you're a skilled alchemist in a hidden laboratory, working with esoteric substances to create a potent elixir. Just as an alchemist transforms one substance into another, we too transform the surrounding energies to manifest our desires. In this alchemical process, intention is our philosopher's stone.

The transmutation of energy in baneful magik involves the careful manipulation of energetic currents to produce a specific outcome. This is not a haphazard process but a precise and deliberate one, akin to a master craftsman shaping a work of art.

Consider the analogy of a blacksmith forging a blade. The blacksmith meticulously heats, hammers, and tempers the metal to create a sharp and resilient weapon. Similarly, in baneful magik, we must understand the nuances of energy manipulation to craft our metaphysical tools effectively.

WORKING THE MAGIK

At this point, you might have been talked out of working baneful magik.

Then again, you might be planning to plow ahead. You've worked out that the target deserves what magik you plan, and this target is responsible for trouble or problems for others. Then you need to craft the correct petition and, from the petition, craft a sigil. Once the ritual is worked, the sigil is activated, and then you wait.

And wait.

And wait some more.

This is because in order to correctly apply the effect you desire may take some arranging on the part of Lucifer Daemonic, and the universe at large.

So, I caution patience. If after 90 days, or three moon cycles, nothing appears to be happening, you can try again. But prior to this, run a ritual to Lucifer Daemonic, and ASK him what is going on. He'll tell you. It might be that you are going after the wrong target after all!

In my experience, when magik fails, it's because a key element is missing or incorrect. Or, you haven't waited long enough.

I had an issue in 2020 with two people, while I was busy launching my occult writing, and I was also busy running some teaching programs. One person was very vocal on all social media that my methods were "dangerous". Yet - it was his so-called magik that was actually very dark and dangerous. So, I worked a brief ritual. The aim was to expose this person as a fraud. The worse possible punishment for this person is to simply expose their fraud. Then, after six months after working the ritual, they were exposed. The so-called "angel" he was asking people to "feed" was actually a true dark entity, and all this person's followers dropped ran away.

That is the best punishment for that type of person.

So, I encourage you to step back and examine the situation from all angles. Then move forward only when you are 100%, fully one-hundred percent positive, they are deserving of treatment from Lucifer the Daemonic.

BANEFUL MAGIK RITUAL TO LUCIFER THE DAEMONIC

Creating a magik ritual that involves baneful magik should always be approached with caution and a strong sense of ethics. Here's a template for a ritual to Lucifer the Daemonic, focusing on baneful magik.

Remember to consider the consequences and ethical implications of your actions before proceeding. This template is a departure from my usual rituals, in that I am instructing you to write the petition and craft the sigil while in ritual. Of course, work out the petition beforehand, making sure it's as brief as possible, and as complete as you can make it.

I also suggest that you select a special set of clothing to wear for this. It's an odd thing, but clothing and cloth can pick up magik energy. For this magik, I suggest you wear clothing just for this ritual, then do a ritual cleansing of these cloths afterward.

We'll be using the traditional ENN for this aspect: Renich Tasa Uberaca Biasa Icar Lucifer.

Items Needed:

Altar candles in all black.

A small chime candle in black.

A piece of parchment paper.

A black ink pen.

A small mirror.

A personal item or representation/photo of the target (if applicable).

Protective amulets or symbols (optional).

Incense (dragon's blood, myrrh, or patchouli are suitable).

A bowl of salt.

A bowl of water.

The ritual:

Preparation: Begin by cleansing yourself and the ritual space. Work a self-purification spell, visualize any negativity leaving you, and dress in clean, dark-colored clothing.

Casting the Circle: Stand in the center of your ritual space and visualize a circle of protection forming around you. Imagine a barrier that prevents negative energies from entering.

Light the Candle: Place the black candle in the center of your circle and light it, saying, "I call upon Lucifer the Daemonic, the guardian of the shadows, to aid me in my quest."

Write Your Intent: On the parchment paper, write your intent in clear, concise words. Be specific about the outcome you desire. Avoid vague or harmful intentions. Fold the paper towards you.

Mirror Symbolism: Place the small mirror in front of the candle. As you look into the mirror, visualize the energy of Lucifer the Daemonic reflecting back at you, amplifying your intent.

Invocation: Say aloud, **"Renich Tasa Uberaca Biasa Icar *Lucifer*! I invoke your presence. I seek your guidance in this endeavor. Assist me in my righteous cause."**

Personal Item or Representation: If you have a personal item or representation of the target, place it in front of the mirror. If not, visualize the target's image as clearly as possible.

Enact the Baneful Magik: Holding the folded parchment paper in one hand, focus your intent on the target or issue. Visualize the desired outcome. As you do so, recite your intent aloud, stating your wishes clearly and with conviction. Feel the energy building within you.

Submerge in Salt: Dip the parchment paper into the bowl of salt, symbolizing the banishing or purification of negative influences.

Cleanse with Water: Dip the parchment paper into

the bowl of water, symbolizing a cleansing of the situation. Imagine the negative energy dissipating.

Final Invocation: Say, "Lucifer the Daemonic, I release this energy into your hands. May it be used for justice and balance. As I will, so mote it be."

Extinguish the Candle: Blow out the black candle, visualizing the energy being sent to fulfill your intent.

Closing the Circle: Thank Lucifer the Daemonic for their assistance and visualize the protective circle dissipating.

Dispose of Materials: Safely dispose of the parchment paper (bury it or burn it) and cleanse the mirror with salt and water.

Grounding: Take a moment to ground yourself by eating or drinking something nourishing.

Always remember to use baneful magik responsibly and ethically, considering the consequences of your actions carefully. Harm none and respect the free will of others.

Unless they really deserve it, you know?

CHAPTER 7

LUCIFER THE FALLEN

A brief and last word about Lucifer. The aspect known as Lucifer the Fallen bears a striking resemblance to the aspect we have just studied, namely Lucifer the Daemonic. When considering everything, it becomes clear that there is very little that distinguishes Lucifer the Egregore from Lucifer the Daemonic, and there are even fewer characteristics that separate the Fallen from these two aspects.

In my opinion, if I were to examine this aspect and offer guidance on rituals to The Fallen, I would be repetitively addressing the same topic. However, it is crucial to mention that the primary purpose of this book was to explore the celestial elements. It is important to note that a thorough examination of Lucifer would not be considered comprehensive unless this aspect is acknowledged to some degree.

The narrative surrounding Lucifer's fall from grace is highly varied and sourced from an array of religious texts, literary works, and occult interpretations. The details and reasons behind this fall are essential, as they greatly influence whether Lucifer is viewed as a tragic hero or an embodiment of evil.

In Christian tradition, the story of Lucifer's fall is most prominently outlined in texts like Isaiah 14 and Ezekiel 28, though these are not explicit in naming Lucifer as the fallen angel. The general consensus among many Christian scholars and theologians is that Lucifer was cast out of Heaven due to his rebellion against God. His sin was that of pride, thinking he could overthrow God and take His place. This narrative sets up Lucifer as the ultimate antagonist, a symbol of pure evil and rebellion against divine authority.

Certain apocryphal texts, like the "Book of Enoch," offer additional perspectives on fallen angels, though Lucifer is not explicitly named. These texts can contribute to a richer understanding of the story of the fallen angels, even if they are not considered canonical by mainstream Christian denominations.

John Milton's "Paradise Lost" is a pivotal work that

explores the story of Lucifer's rebellion in great detail. In this epic poem, Lucifer is portrayed as a tragic hero who rebels against what he perceives as the tyranny of God. His famous declaration, "Better to reign in Hell than serve in Heaven," has significantly influenced the perception of Lucifer as a symbol of individualism and resistance against authoritarian power.

In Dante Alighieri's "Inferno," Lucifer is portrayed as the ultimate sinner, trapped in the frozen lake at the center of Hell. Unlike Milton's portrayal, Dante's Lucifer is less a tragic hero and more of a cautionary figure who embodies the perils of defying divine authority.

In various occult traditions, the narrative around Lucifer's fall takes on more nuanced meanings. For instance, in certain Gnostic traditions, Lucifer's act of rebellion is seen not as a malicious act but as a quest for enlightenment and freedom from a malevolent or ignorant Demiurge, the creator of the material world. Similarly, in Thelemic and Luciferian traditions, Lucifer is often seen as a liberator who brings the light of knowledge to humanity, not unlike Prometheus in Greek mythology.

Today, some neo-pagan and modern occult practices honor Lucifer as a misunderstood or misrepresented deity who champions individual empowerment and spiritual awakening. The idea is that the traditional narrative of

Lucifer's fall may have been a way to demonize pre-Christian gods or perspectives that emphasized individuality over communal. This alternative interpretation of Lucifer seeks to challenge the conventional understanding of his role as a malevolent figure. Instead, it posits him as a symbol of personal liberation and enlightenment. In neo-pagan and modern occult circles, Lucifer is seen as a deity who encourages individuals to embrace their own power and follow their own spiritual paths.

Advocates of this viewpoint argue that the traditional narrative of Lucifer's fall from grace may have been a deliberate attempt to vilify ancient gods or belief systems that celebrated individuality and self-determination. By associating these perspectives with a malevolent figure, communal obedience and conformity were promoted as the preferred values.

By reclaiming Lucifer as a misunderstood deity, these neo-pagan and modern occult practices aim to challenge societal norms and encourage individuals to embrace their unique identities and spiritual journeys. They see Lucifer as a force that breaks free from the constraints of dogma and encourages personal growth and empowerment.

It is important to note that these interpretations of Lucifer vary among different neo-pagan and modern occult traditions. Some may view Lucifer as a literal entity, while others perceive him as a symbolic representation of inner rebellion and self-discovery. Nonetheless, the overarching theme is to embrace personal autonomy and spiritual awakening, challenging the notion of Lucifer as purely evil and embracing a more nuanced understanding of his role in mythology and spirituality.

In sum, the story of how Lucifer fell—and why—varies significantly, depending on the source. Whether cast as a villain deserving of eternal punishment or a tragic hero fighting against cosmic injustice, each interpretation offers a unique lens through which to explore this enigmatic figure.

I went over the real reason Lucifer, and others, "fell" in the previous chapter on Lucifer, the Creator God. Thus, his "falling" was done out of love for the early humans and to make sure the experiment was conducted without failure.

Leveraging the magik of this aspect is easily done using the following simple ritual:

THE ILLUMINATION RITUAL

This ritual is designed to seek illumination, insight, and guidance from Lucifer the Fallen, who is often seen as a symbol of enlightenment and resistance against oppressive forces. It's a ritual for those who wish to embrace their own inner light and question established norms.

This ritual can be modified to ask Lucifer, the Fallen, most any question, or to present a petition if you feel you resonate with this aspect.

Items Needed:

A black candle (representing Lucifer's fallen nature).

A white candle (symbolizing illumination and purity).

Lucifer's Fallen Angelic Sigil

A small offering, such as a piece of dark chocolate or a glass of red wine.

Incense of any type. Stick or resin. If using resin, go with frankincense and dragon's blood.

Ritual Steps:

Cast a simple circle.

Place the black candle on your left side and the white candle on your right side. Light both candles. Sit comfortably in front of them.

Invocation: Close your eyes, take several deep breaths, and center yourself.

Now say:

Lucifer the Fallen, Lightbringer of the Morning Star,

I stand before you with reverence and awe.

I seek your presence, not out of arrogance or vanity,

But to gain wisdom and insight from your boundless clarity.

Lucifer, I summon you from realms untold,
In the name of my purpose, my spirit, my soul.
With the utmost respect and pure intent,
I ask that you join me, as our energies blend.

Lucifer, I welcome you with an open heart,
May our connection be a work of sacred art.
So mote it be, this pact we create,
In your name, Lucifer, I consecrate."

Question: Now, in your mind or out loud, ask Lucifer the Fallen a specific question or request guidance on a particular aspect of your life. Be clear and concise in your inquiry.

Meditation: Relax and focus on the flickering flames

of the black and white candles. Imagine the duality and balance they represent. Visualize a gentle, radiant light emerging from the white candle and illuminating your path.

Listening: As you meditate, be open to receiving insights, images, or words that come to your mind. Lucifer the Fallen may communicate with you in subtle ways. Trust your intuition.

Offering: Pick up the small offering you've prepared. Offer it to Lucifer by saying, **"Lucifer the Fallen, I offer this token of appreciation for your guidance and illumination."** Place the offering in front of the candles.

Closing: Extinguish the candles in reverse order, starting with the white one and then the black one. As you do, imagine that you carry the wisdom and illumination you've received with you into your daily life.

Journaling: After the ritual, take a few moments to jot down any insights, feelings, or images you received during the meditation. This will help you remember and integrate the guidance you've received.

Reflection: In the days following the ritual, pay

attention to any signs, synchronicities, or shifts in your perspective. Lucifer the Fallen may continue to offer guidance and illumination in unexpected ways.

Remember that this ritual is a personal and spiritual experience, and your connection with Lucifer the Fallen may evolve over time. Approach it with an open heart and a sincere desire for illumination and insight.

Dispose of the offering as instructed previously.

CHAPTER 8

PACTS

What is a Pact?

In magik, a pact is a sacred contract or agreement established between a practitioner and a spiritual entity, often a deity, demon, or other supernatural being. Pacts are symbolic and binding agreements that outline specific terms, conditions, and expectations between the two parties involved. These agreements are not to be taken lightly; they represent a profound commitment and exchange of energies.

At the heart of a pact lies a mutual exchange. The practitioner offers something of value, such as devotion, service, offerings, or loyalty, in exchange for assistance, guidance, knowledge, or power from the spiritual entity. This exchange is a fundamental principle in various magikal traditions, and pacts are a tangible expression of this reciprocity.

When to Form a Pact?

The decision to enter into a pact is a significant one in the practice of magik. It's essential to understand when and why such agreements are typically made:

Seeking Knowledge and Wisdom: One common reason to establish a pact is to gain access to hidden or esoteric knowledge. Practitioners may desire insights into the mysteries of the universe, the secrets of the spirit world, or the nature of reality. Entities like Lucifer, known for their profound wisdom, are often sought for such pacts.

Acquiring Power and Abilities: Another motivation is to acquire specific powers or capabilities beyond the ordinary. This could involve enhancing one's psychic faculties, gaining control over natural elements, or accessing spiritual protection. Spirits with expertise in these areas can be approached for such pacts.

Aid in Spiritual or Life Challenges: Some practitioners turn to pacts when faced with significant challenges in their lives or spiritual journeys. Seeking guidance, protection, or solutions to problems is a valid reason to enter into an agreement with a spiritual entity.

Dedicating to a Deity or Entity: In some magikal traditions, individuals may choose to make a pact as an act of devotion and dedication to a specific deity or spirit. This can involve committing to a lifelong relationship and service.

Exploring One's Path: Pacts can also be made as a means of exploring one's spiritual path and deepening one's connection with the spiritual realms. For those on a quest for self-discovery, a pact can be a transformative experience.

How to Work a Pact with Lucifer:

Research and Preparation: Before initiating contact with Lucifer or any other spiritual entity, thorough research is paramount. Understand the entity's nature, attributes, and the historical or mythological context in which they are revered. Preparation may include purification rituals, meditation, and crafting offerings or gifts.

Clearly define your intentions and the terms of the pact. What are you seeking from Lucifer, and what are you willing to offer in return? Be specific and precise in your requests to avoid misunderstandings.

Choose an appropriate time and place for the ritual. Create a sacred and protected space for your interaction. Use invocations, prayers, or chants to call upon Lucifer respectfully and with reverence. Maintain an open and receptive state of mind to receive guidance or messages.

State your commitment and offer your part of the exchange. This might involve promises of devotion, service, or specific actions. Lucifer may convey their expectations or guidance to you. Once both parties agree to the terms, consider sealing the pact symbolically, such as through a physical object or written agreement.

Fulfill your part of the pact diligently and with sincerity. Do your part. Maintain your end of the agreement, whether through offerings, regular rituals, or acts of service. This demonstrates your commitment and strengthens the bond.

Maintain open lines of communication with Lucifer. Regular meditation, prayer, or rituals can help foster a deep and ongoing connection. Seek guidance, wisdom, or assistance as needed and show gratitude for any assistance received.

Always approach the pact with respect and ethical consideration. Avoid using the pact for harmful or malicious purposes, as this can lead to negative consequences. Uphold your end of the agreement with integrity.

Working a pact with a spirit like Lucifer can be a transformative and enlightening experience. It requires dedication, understanding, and a profound respect for the spiritual realms. As with any magikal practice, approach it with discernment and a sincere desire for personal and spiritual growth.

Writing the Pact

A pact statement is a lot like a petition, except it's worded as if it's a contact.

- Be specific about what you will offer and when.
- Be specific about what you expect from the spirit.

Although you can use my sample, it's best to word it such that it matches your own words. Draw a sigil for the spirit at the bottom of the pact, or your desire sigil. Sometimes, a spirit will enter into a pact, and nothing happens. At the end of the pact, you will run a final ritual of gratitude in which you also dissolve the pact. If Lucifer fails on his end of the pact, run a ritual to ask him why he's not fulfilling his end of the pact. There could be one of many reasons the pact magik is not working. You won't know unless you ask Lucifer.

If you have a difficult time hearing Lucifer, use a pendulum and answer board to hear him, or use Tarot cards.

SAMPLE PACT STATEMENT

Suggested way to craft the pact:

I, ______________________ in deepest respect and admiration, hereby call upon the [God's Name] and humbly offer up to him [what you are offering] in exchange for [what you want].

I affirm that a pact with you, [Name], is my most heartfelt desire. I dedicate myself to [how you wish to change or live].

By signing below, I do dedicate myself to [what you wish to become or have happen for you.]

Below I offer my signature:

Offerings

With pacts, keep the offerings as simple as possible. For any aspect, a small libation works quite well. Go with red wine, or a decent whiskey or spirit.

THE PACT RITUAL

Work the Pact ritual the same as a normal ritual.

- Have your pre-written pact with you, as well as a bottle of magik ink and a pen.

- Open the ritual as previously instructed. Summon the spirit.
- Read your pact out loud.
- If possible, wait a moment for the spirit to reply.
- VISUALIZE the outcome.
- Sign the pact with the magik ink. If this is a Daemonic Pact, a drop of blood will work like a signature.
- Do a small offering.
- At this point, end the ritual, or burn the pact, then end the ritual.
    - It's debated which works best. My experience shows no difference in the ultimate outcome.

During the Pact's term:

- Work weekly rituals to check in on the spirit working the pact.
- During which, visualize the outcome.
- A small offering to the spirit.

DO NOT try to change the pact! If you've changed your mind, run a Pact Dissolution ritual.

If there is no movement on the pact, nothing even hinting at manifesting, run a ritual to make contact and use a pendulum or Tarot to see what's holding it up.

If the desire has occurred, or the pact isn't working at all, run the Pact Dissolve ritual.

PACT DISSOLVE RITUAL

Work this under the following situations: The pact has manifested and is no longer needed, or the spirit isn't doing anything and you need to "Fire" the spirit.

Set up as usual with the pact you wish to dissolve (or a copy) on the altar.

Open the ritual as usual, and summon the spirit.

IF dissolving a non-functioning pact, let the spirit KNOW why it's being dissolved. It might be issues beyond anyone's control.

If the pact has manifest, give the usual offering of thanks.

Close as usual. Dispose of the offering as usual.

WEEKLY GRATITUDE RITUALS

While in a pact, it's advisable to run a simple ritual once a week, to give thanks to Lucifer in which ever aspect you chose for a pact.

This is a simplified ritual, with minimal tools.

Depending on which aspect you chose to enter into a

pact with, you will need to work a simple ritual each week.

SIMPLE GRATITUDE RITUAL

Set up your altar space. Minimal tools or props.

Summon the spirit. Use the corresponding sigil for this ritual.

Make the offering. The offering will vary by ritual and spirit.

Close the ritual in the usual manner.

Again: wait overnight or 24 hrs, then dispose of the offering.

CHAPTER 9

LUCIFER SIGILS

What follows are the new sigils I created for this book. Each sigil is intimately tied to that aspect of Lucifer.

Although I have energized these sigils in ritual before this book was published, you still need to work a small activation on each one yourself. This ties your energy to that of the sigil, making it much more effective.

This ritual is simple, and can be easily done while in a ritual to an aspect of Lucifer. Just do this before summoning Lucifer in your ritual.

During a ritual, pause after establishing the circle, and pick up the sigil. Trace over it with your index finger, either hand, doesn't matter, going over the lines in the sigil. Imagine in your head the lines beginning to glow with energy. As your finger traces over the lines, the lines glow with energy.

Allow the glowing lines to slowly fade away, leaving the original black lines of the sigil.

In a separate mini-ritual, just light a candle and establish a simple circle. Then repeat the steps from earlier, activating the sigil for use. In a standalone ritual, you can activate every sigil in this book at the same time.

I recommend energizing each sigil each time you print one out.

Lightbringer

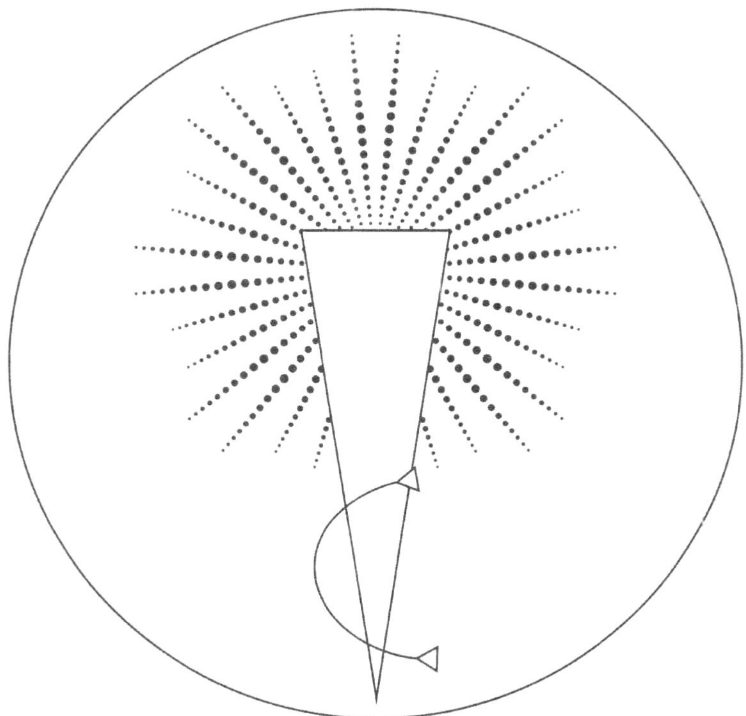

Lucifer Creator God

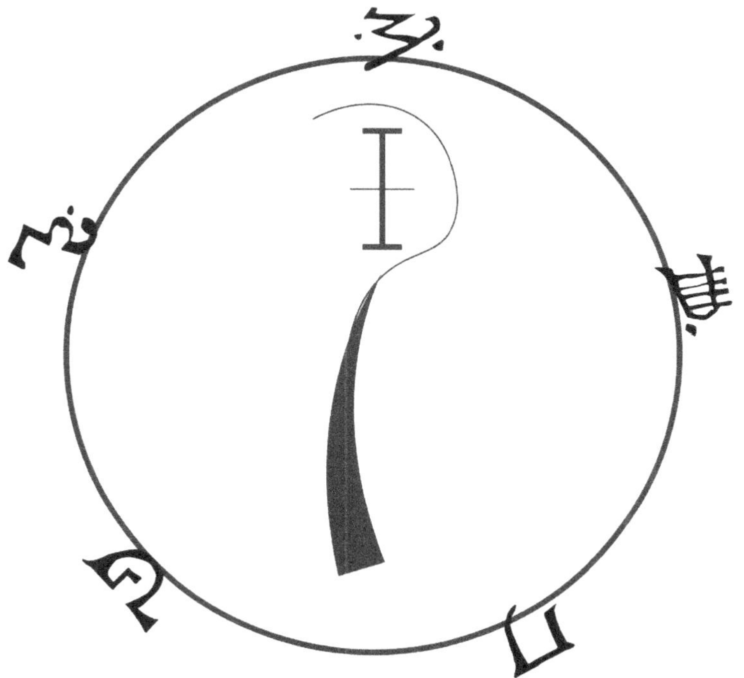

Lucifer Egregore

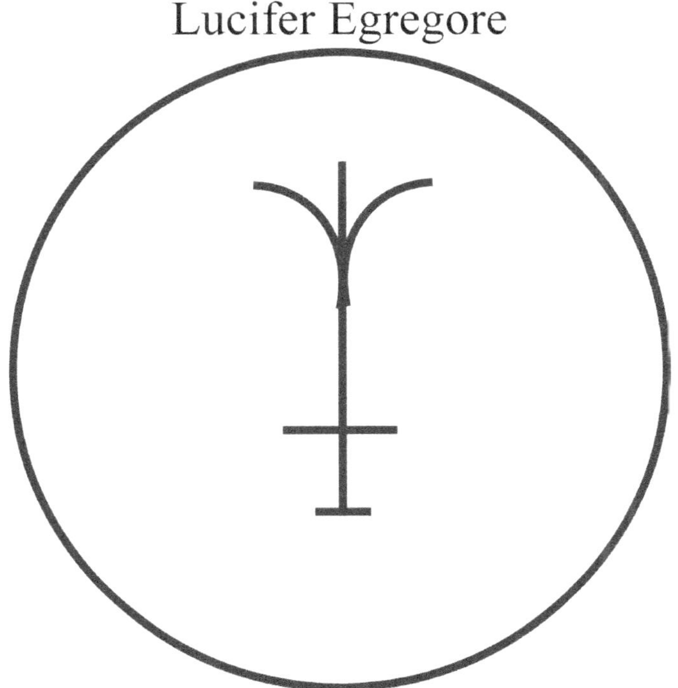

Lucifer Daemon Traditional

Lucifer Daemonic

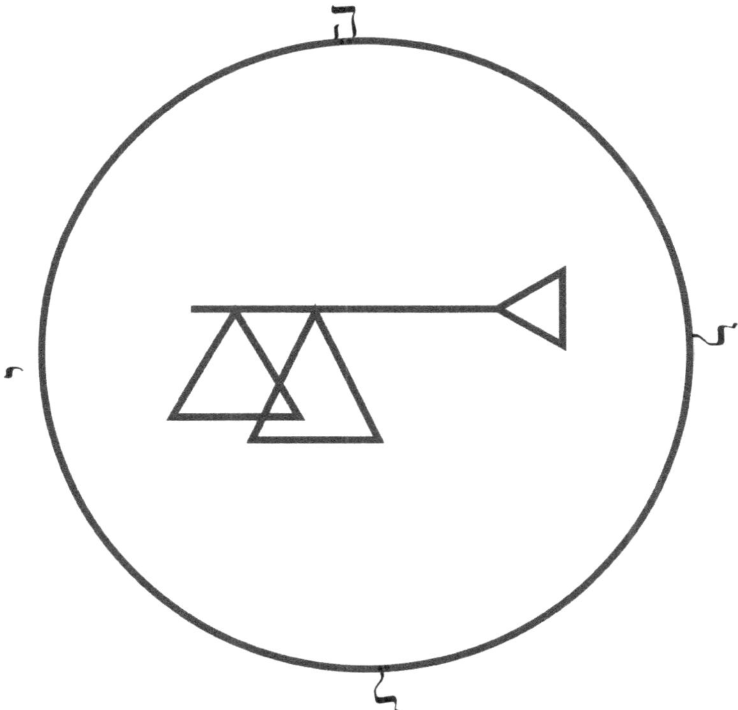

Lucifer the Fallen

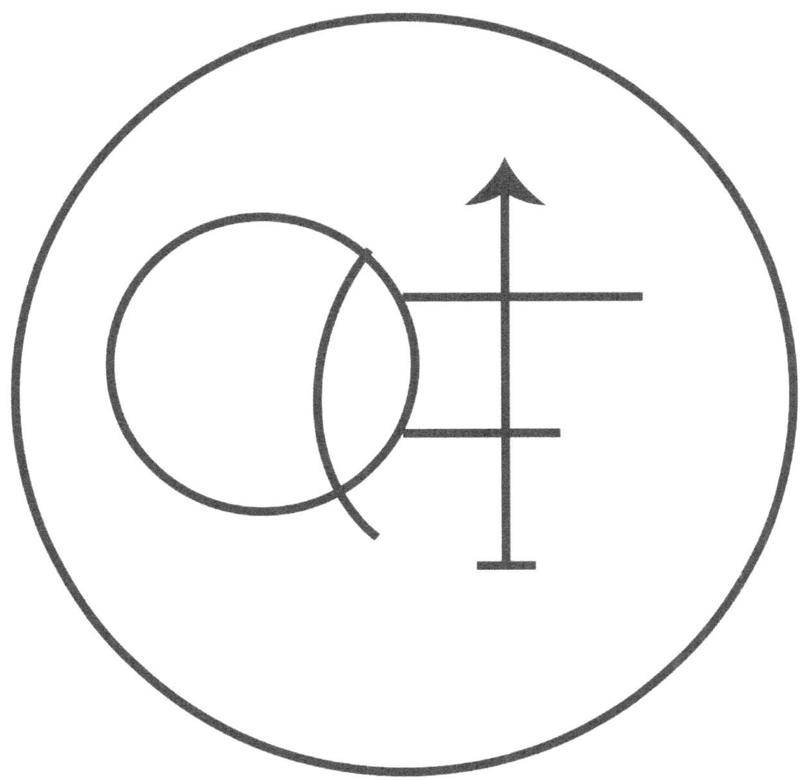

APPENDIX

Helpful Links:

My Sigil Course:
https://highmagikacademy.com/courses-page/sigil-basics-and-worksheets/

Sigils found in this book:
https://davepsychic.com/lucifer-book-sigils/

Color Correspondences

Colors serve as potent visual cues to focus your intent and channel energies into your spells or rituals. Here's a basic guide to some common colors and their traditional meanings within the context of magik and spell craft:

Red

Magical Properties: Passion, love, strength, courage

Best Used: Love spells, increasing personal power,

courage rituals

Orange

Magical Properties: Creativity, energy, attraction, stimulation

Best Used: Creativity spells, attraction spells, energizing rituals

Yellow

Magical Properties: Wisdom, communication, clarity, happiness

Best Used: Divination, inspiration spells, learning and studying aids

Green

Magical Properties: Prosperity, fertility, healing, growth

Best Used: Money spells, fertility rituals, healing work

Blue

Magical Properties: Calm, truth, communication, psychic awareness

Best Used: Calming spells, truth spells, psychic development

Purple

Magical Properties: Power, spiritual connection, wisdom

Best Used: Spiritual enlightenment, connection to higher powers, wisdom rituals

Pink

Magical Properties: Love, friendship, emotional healing

Best Used: Love spells, friendship rituals, emotional balancing spells

Black

Magical Properties: Protection, banishment, absorbing negativity

Best Used: Protection spells, banishing rituals, uncrossing spells

White

Magical Properties: Purity, cleansing, peace, unity

Best Used: Cleansing rituals, peace spells, general-purpose magik

Brown

Magical Properties: Stability, grounding, practicality

Best Used: Grounding spells, stability rituals, practical endeavors

Gray

Magical Properties: Neutrality, balance, veiling

Best Used: Neutralizing negative influences, balance, veiling spells

Gold

Magical Properties: Wealth, success, higher spiritual understanding

Best Used: Money spells, success rituals, higher spiritual workings

Silver

Magical Properties: Intuition, emotional balance, lunar connections

Best Used: Moon rituals, intuitive development, balancing emotions

You can customize this list based on your own experiences and intuition, as you use colors in your magik, you may notice specific shifts in the meanings.

SIMPLE CIRCLE CASTING

Items needed (optional)

4 Elemental symbols or objects (e.g., feather/incense smoke for Air, candle for Fire, cup of water for Water, pentacle or salt for Earth)

Steps:

Cleanse the Area: Before you begin, make sure your ritual space is clean and free from distractions. I use frankincense to purify the atmosphere in my ritual space.

Center Yourself: Take a few deep breaths, grounding

yourself in the present moment.

Begin the Circle: Starting at the East, use your wand, athame, or pointed finger to draw the circle around you. Visualize a circle of protective light emerging as you move.

Call the East (Air): Place your Air symbol in the East direction, then say, *"Guardians of the East, spirits of Air, I call upon you to watch over this circle. Lend me your intellect and clarity."*

Call the South (Fire): Place your Fire symbol in the South direction, then say, *"Guardians of the South, spirits of Fire, I call upon you to watch over this circle. Lend me your passion and energy."*

Call the West (Water): Place your Water symbol in the West direction, then say, *"Guardians of the West, spirits of Water, I call upon you to watch over this circle. Lend me your intuition and emotional wisdom."*

Call the North (Earth): Place your Earth symbol in the North direction, then say, "Guardians of the North, spirits of Earth, I call upon you to watch over this circle. Lend me your strength and stability."

Seal the Circle: Return to the East and complete your circle by saying, "The circle is now cast, and we stand between the worlds. May this space be a sanctuary for magick and transformation."

Perform Your Ritual: With the circle cast and guardians called, you are now ready to proceed with your intended magickal workings.

Close the Circle: Once you've completed your ritual, thank each guardian starting from the North and moving in reverse order, releasing them and their energies. Then visualize the circle dissipating, signifying the end of the ritual space.

DAEMONIC CIRCLE CASTING AND SUMMONING

Traditional circle casting when using any daemon, and Lucifer in his Daemonic or Egregore aspect.

Please note that the following is a traditional example, but many practitioners adapt it to fit their personal styles and beliefs. Always exercise caution and ensure you fully understand the ethics and safety concerns surrounding daemonic magick.

It is vital you work the protection summonings when

casting a circle to summon a daemonic being. Especially Lucifer.

Preparations:

Cleanse and Consecrate the Space: Before casting the circle, cleanse the area of negative energies using frankincense, saltwater, or other purifying methods.

Gather Tools: Typically, you will need a wand or athame, a chalice of water, a dish of salt, a feather or incense smoking, and a lit candle to represent the four elements.

Defining the Circle: Some people like to physically draw a circle, if so, use chalk or salt to physically draw the circle on the floor or ground of your space.

Casting the Circle:

Stand in the Circle: Enter the circle, facing East. Close your eyes and take a deep breath to center yourself.

Call Upon the Guardians: Lift your wand or athame and begin by facing each cardinal direction as you invoke the guardians or daemons of each element.

East (Air): "I call upon the daemons of Air, masters

of intellect and thought, to guard this circle and witness my rite."

South (Fire): "I call upon the daemons of Fire, keepers of will and transformation, to guard this circle and witness my rite."

West (Water): "I call upon the daemons of Water, rulers of emotion and intuition, to guard this circle and witness my rite."

North (Earth): "I call upon the daemons of Earth, stewards of foundation and physical form, to guard this circle and witness my rite."

Seal the Circle: After calling all four elements, raise your tool of choice above your head and visualize a sphere of light forming around you. Declare, "The circle is sealed, and this space is sacred."

Performing the Ritual:

Now your circle is cast, and you may proceed with your ritual, secure in the knowledge that you are protected and the energies you call upon are contained.

Closing the Circle:

Thank the Guardians: Facing each direction once more, thank the elemental daemons for their presence and assistance, asking them to depart in peace.

Seal the Portal: Declare, "This circle is open, but never broken," visualizing the energy dispersing back into the world.

Clean Up: Erase or dismantle any physical representations of the circle.

Remember that these are guidelines and can be adapted as you see fit for yourself and your practice of magik. Always exercise caution and make sure you're well-read and well-prepared before performing any ritual.

RITUAL CLEANSING

Before working some magik, and, especially after working any baneful magik, it is suggested you do a cleanse afterwards. Clothing tends to soak up energy, and energy like baneful magik can build up and eventually cause issues.

This is really simple. No need to make a huge fuss over this.

After working the magik, take the clothing you were

wearing and pass it carefully through incense smoke, or lay it out in the purifying rays of the sun. I recommend using frankincense for this.

And no, don't simply wear your clothes outside in the sun. Spread them out on a table or railing, allowing the full sun to shine on the cloths. After 30 minutes, turn them over, or move them around, so that each side gets at least 30 minutes of sunlight.

That's all there is to this.

Also, if you have slightly yellowed white clothing, the sun will also help return it to its original brightness. My granny taught me this when I was a kid. It was one of the effects of hanging your laundry in the air to dry, versus using a clothes dryer.

For cleansing yourself after a magik session, or just prior, I suggest filling your bath with some hot water, and drop in some Florida water. It's found online, and can be made quite easily by combining 91% isopropyl alcohol with some citrus essential oils and rose water. After soaking a bit, including your head, stand up and hang out in the bathroom to allow yourself to air dry.

Again, quite easy and there's no reason to make a more elaborate deal about this.

SIMPLE GRATITUDE RITUAL

A simple ritual, designed to be worked when it's apparent the magik is working, and your desire is manifesting.

Items needed:

A single white candle

Lucifer's sigil for whatever aspect you used.

Offering & offering bowl

THE SIMPLIFIED LESSER BANISHING RITUAL OF THE PENTAGRAM

Preparation:

Find a quiet and undisturbed space.

Stand upright with your feet together, arms relaxed at your sides.

Step 1: Relaxation

Close your eyes and take several deep breaths.

Imagine a brilliant white light above you, cleansing and purifying.

As you exhale, visualize any tension leaving your body and flowing down into the Earth.

Step 2: The Qabalistic Cross

Touch your forehead and say, "Ateh" (Thine is).

Touch your chest and say, "Malkuth" (The Kingdom).

Touch your right shoulder and say, "ve-Geburah" (and the Power).

Touch your left shoulder and say, "ve-Gedulah" (and the Glory).

Clasp your hands at your chest and say, "le-Olahm, Amen" (Forever, Amen).

Step 3: The Pentagrams

Stand facing east. With your right index finger or wand, visualize a brilliant white light.

Draw a large banishing Earth pentagram in the east while vibrating "YHVH" (Yod-Heh-Vav-Heh).

See the pentagram glowing with white light.

Turn to the south, draw another pentagram, and vibrate "Adonai" (Ah-doh-nye).

See the pentagram glowing with white light.

Turn to the west, draw a pentagram, and vibrate "Eheieh" (Eh-heh-yeh).

See the pentagram glowing with white light.

Turn to the north, draw a pentagram, and vibrate "Agla" (Ah-glah).

See the pentagram glowing with white light.

Return to the east, completing the circle of

pentagrams.

Step 4: The Closing Qabalistic Cross

Stand with your arms outstretched and feet together.

Visualize a brilliant white light above your head.

Say, "Ateh Malkuth ve-Geburah ve-Gedulah le-Olahm, Amen."

Cross your arms over your chest, right over left, and say, "Le-Olahm, Amen."

Conclusion:

Take a moment to breathe and visualize the brilliance of the white light surrounding you.

Close the ritual with gratitude and a sense of protection.

This simplified version retains the essence of the Lesser Banishing Ritual of the Pentagram while making it accessible for beginners. As you become more comfortable with it, you can incorporate additional elements and visualizations to deepen your practice.

GLOSSARY OF TERMS

Aspect: Different facets or representations of a deity or spiritual entity, each with its own characteristics and attributes.

Baneful Magic: Magical practices focused on causing harm or disruption, often associated with negative consequences if used irresponsibly.

Blow-Back: Negative consequences or backlash that may result from certain magical practices, especially baneful magic.

Communal Obedience: Adherence to group or societal

norms and rules at the expense of individuality and personal freedom.

Daemon: A spiritual entity or supernatural being, often associated with guidance or assistance in magical practices.

Demiurge: In Gnostic traditions, a lower deity responsible for creating the material world, often seen as ignorant or malevolent.

Egregore: A collective consciousness or psychic entity created and sustained by the beliefs and emotions of a group of individuals.

Gods and Goddesses: Deities from various mythologies and religious traditions, often invoked in rituals and magical workings.

Gnostic Traditions: Philosophical and religious beliefs that emphasize direct mystical experience and knowledge as a path to salvation or enlightenment.

Lucifer: An enigmatic figure with various aspects, including the Daemonic, Egregore, and Fallen, often invoked in occult and magical practices.

Magik: A term used to refer to magical practices, often associated with the occult and esoteric traditions.

Neo-Pagan: Contemporary pagan or nature-based religious movements often drawing inspiration from ancient pagan traditions.

Pathworking: A guided visualization or meditation technique used to explore spiritual realms and connect with spiritual entities.

Petition: A statement or request made to a spiritual entity or deity in magical workings.

Prometheus: In Greek mythology, a figure who defied the gods to bring knowledge and fire to humanity, often seen as a symbol of enlightenment and rebellion.

Sigil: A symbol or design created to represent a specific intention or desire in magical rituals.

Thelemic Tradition: A spiritual and philosophical system founded by Aleister Crowley, emphasizing individual will and spiritual evolution.

Tragic Hero: A character, often in literature, who possesses noble qualities but experiences a downfall due to a tragic flaw or external circumstances.

ABOUT THE AUTHOR

Dave is an author of adult fantasy (The Furies series) as well as author of occult books about magick.

He began working ritual magick back in the 1970s. He took a brief break, then used the power of this magick to create a photography career which took him to Los Angeles and work as a photographer for multiple magazines.

David has studied magick in all forms, and in 2018, released a three-part magick instruction course in High Magick. Thousands of students have benefited from David's unique teaching style, making ceremonial magick accessible to everyone.

This book on Lucifer is number 11 in his High Magick Series.

Dave also has a series on Grecian Magick, exploring the aspects of ceremonial magick with the gods and goddesses of ancient Greece.

Dave's Facebook Page:
https://www.facebook.com/DavePsychic/

Secrets of Magick Facebook Group:
https://www.facebook.com/groups/secretsofmagick

Join the Grecian Magick Facebook group!
https://www.facebook.com/groups/grecianmagick

Dave's webpage, book readings and his services:
https://davepsychic.com
Then his e-learning website for magik classes
https://highmagikacademy.com

Magick Books by David Thompson

Available as EPUB, Paperback and Hardcover (*)

High Magick Series

- High Magick 101
- Daemons of High Magick

- Daemons and the Law of Attraction*
- Magick of Astaroth*
- Lilith: Goddess of Darkness and Light*
- Daemons of Fortune*
- Asmodeus, King of Daemons*
- Goddesses of High Magick
- Protection Magik
- The Diviner's Handbook
- The Magik of Lucifer*

Grecian Magick Series

- Magick of Apollo
- Magick of Hermes
- Magick of Aphrodite
- Magick of Fortuna*
- Greco-Roman Wealth Magick*
- Magick of the Sirens/Magick of the Muses
- Hermes and the Akashic Records

Fiction Novels by David Thompson

The Furies Series

- Angels of Vengeance
- Descent into Tartarus

- Furies: Beginnings
- Brianna: Making of a Fury

www.ingramcontent.com/pod-product-compliance
Lightning Source LLC
Chambersburg PA
CBHW071325120626
46546CB00002B/438

* 9 7 8 1 9 6 1 7 6 5 1 6 0 *